PACIFIC MARITIME HISTORY SERIES

Number 2

Published by the
ASSOCIATES OF THE NATIONAL MARITIME
MUSEUM LIBRARY
and
THE GLENCANNON PRESS

T0025790

THE VOYAGES
OF THE
SHIP *REVERE*
1849-1883

BY

Madeleine Rowse Gleason

Associates of the National Maritime Museum Library
Pacific Maritime History Series

1994

Pacific Maritime History Series
Number Two

Published by the Glencannon Press
P.O. Box 341, Palo Alto, CA 94302

10 9 8 7 6 5 4 3 2 1

Library of Congress Catalog Card Number 94-075378

ISBN 0-9637586-2-4

For Donald Howes Gleason II
and
Jonathan and Kerin

In memory of
Edward Rowse Gleason
1947-1970

Contents

FOREWORD

The Associates of the National Maritime Museum Library are pleased to bring out as joint publisher this second of the Pacific Maritime History Series. David A. Hull, Principal Librarian of the J. Porter Shaw Library at the National Maritime Museum, San Francisco, and a founder of the Associates, observed in his preface to our first volume, "Scammon," that publishing is an integral part of the Museum's function of preserving and documenting its collections.

Probably no other development in modern maritime history compares to the burgeoning of coastwise and deep water trade on our Pacific Coast beginning in 1849. Mr. Hull described the transformation of our sleepy coastal waters into major new ports and seaways, busy with our own vessels and foreign flags coming and going, and wrote then: "The aim of the Pacific Maritime History Series is to publish maritime history relating to the Pacific Coast and the Pacific Basin, . . . From the great stores of this library as well as from other sources, the Associates expect to publish first-hand accounts by the men and women who sailed the ships, who caught the fish, who lived their lives upon the sea."

Our aim remains the same as we begin here a collaboration with The Glencannon Press, in which we look forward to publishing at shorter intervals. With confidence and pleasure, we begin the collaboration with this scholarly work of Mrs. Madeleine Rowse Gleason, introduced by the distinguished maritime historian, Captain Harold D. Huycke.

We are grateful to the Boston Marine Society for their interest and support and thank the following for their assistance in this project: Steve Canright, Peter Evans, David A. Hull, Harold D. Huycke, Walter W. Jaffee, and Bob Parkinson.

Graydon S. Staring, President
Associates of the National
Maritime Museum Library

PREFACE

An oil painting of the ship *Revere* has come down through three generations of descendants of Osborn Howes, the Boston merchant whose firm commissioned the building of the vessel. It has evoked little more curiosity than any other single picture that might have hung in Grandma Howes' dining room forever. The known facts about the vessel were few: she had been built in 1849 by Hayden & Cudworth in Medford, Massachusetts, for Howes & Crowell, Boston shipping merchants. The chief partners of the firm, great-grandfather Howes and his brother-in-law Nathan Crowell, sold out their interest in the *Revere* in 1862, and her end came in 1883 when she was shipwrecked in the Strait of Juan de Fuca, half a mile west of San Juan harbor in British Columbia.

The project for a history of the ship evolved from an effort to establish a date for the painting, once it had been satisfactorily attributed to a particular painter. Samuel Walters of Liverpool was generally credited as being the artist, although some experts preferred Duncan McFarlane, a younger painter also working in Liverpool in the 1840s and 1850s. One of the Howes descendants, basing his conclusions mainly on artistic arguments, noting two possible McFarlane "trademarks"—the seagull and the floating log in the right foreground of the painting—has opted firmly for McFarlane. The Liverpool docks are recognizable in the background, and the Mersey River entrance in the foreground. Osborn Howes' son observed that the figure "on the quarter deck looking through his spyglass" at the docks was Frederic Howes, the first "commander" of the *Revere*, who must, then, have been at Liverpool with the ship on at least one occasion—unless, of course, the artist used a stock backdrop upon which to paint any vessel wherever such a commission presented itself.

An undated poster in the State Street Trust Company Historical Collection in Boston bears witness to the fact that the *Revere* had indeed been at Liverpool with Frederic Howes as master. She was advertised as one of the packet ships "sailing from Boston semi-monthly and from Liverpool every week," despatched in the Enoch Train line. But when? And what other ports might she have visited in her thirty-four years afloat? These questions were tantalizing enough to launch the research into the ship's history.

The chronicle of the ship's routes immediately provided some answers. The date of the portrait can be postulated as between May 1850 and November 1851, a period during which Frederic Howes was master for five passages to Liverpool. Later voyages, under other masters, would take her to other ports around the world. It soon became apparent that the Boston years encompassed less than half of the ship's sailing life; in later years San Francisco was her home port.

Almost as compelling as the need to date the painting became the need to bring to light the unusual richness and variety of the surviving documents about the *Revere*. Not only are there contemporary newspaper accounts and the usual official records in the National Archives—registers and enrollments, cargo and crew lists, bills of sale and the final wreck report, as well as reports from numerous foreign consular posts—there were also the personal logs of the captain for the first eight voyages in the Atlantic, some financial statements to shareholders, and the papers of Kentfield & Co., owners of the *Revere* from 1865 to the end of her career.

For her first round-the-world voyage, in 1852-53, the captain's official log and a Maury weather-log have survived, as have several letters written by a passenger on the first leg of that trip, from Boston to San Francisco, and published as they were received in a Boston newspaper.

If the documentation seems inordinately detailed, it is because of a conscious effort on the part of the author to introduce other historians of nineteenth-century sailing ships to the variety of resources that are stored in archives, public and private, and in collections all around the country and accessible to any researcher.

The history of the *Revere* is presented in varying fashion depending on the source materials documenting her voyages. For instance, the first eight voyages are detailed because the author had access to Frederic Howes' private journal describing his eight voyages as captain of the vessel. This is a more personal account than the stereotyped ship's log and offers a sense of immediacy that is missing for most of the other voyages. By comparison, the voyages from 1865 on were nearly on a time-table, and generally uneventful. For them a tabulation suffices to give routine information on dates, ports-of-call, consignees, names of occasional passengers, and remarks on the weather. Yet many later voyages are described—because of their unusual routes, or because financial statements have survived that throw light on the economic aspects of the cargo business, or detail the story of a disaster.

For all of Osborn Howes' descendants, East and West, now down to the seventh generation—some in California, some in Arizona, one family in Australia, but most having remained on, or returned to, the East Coast—and likewise for the descendants of Nathan Crowell, of the other shareowners, and of Captain Frederic Howes and the masters who succeeded him, it is my hope that this account of all the *Revere* voyages will be of special interest as the saga of a single vessel in an ancestor's fleet of merchant sail, from her Medford cradle to her grave in the Strait of Juan de Fuca.

Lexington, Massachusetts
April 23, 1994

ACKNOWLEDGMENTS

In the early 1670s Spinoza propounded the theory that intellectual nature abhors a vacuum, and it was surely a great, yawning vacuum that confronted me in the 1970s as I began the quest for the *Revere*'s dates at Liverpool. Happily, not much time elapsed before help came from Frances Gregory, then at work on her book, *Nathan Appleton: Merchant and Entrepreneur*, who recommended the detailed maritime news contained in the *Boston Shipping and Commercial List*. Hard, original copies of the newspaper—in mammoth bound volumes—were available at the New England Deposit Library in nearby Brighton, and the hunt was on.

When it became apparent that the *Revere*'s travels took her far beyond Liverpool and all over the world, I turned to the reference staff in Harvard's Widener Library for guidance. They went immediately to the *Guide to the National Archives of the United States*, which in turn led me to the treasures in Washington. Thanks especially to the expertise and cooperation of staff-member John Vandereedt in the Bureau of Customs collections, I was able to unearth details that I would never have imagined to be extant. And in the Waltham branch of the Archives, Jim Owens alerted me to the microfilms of the Maury logs that had recently been accessioned, and I had the dubious honor of being the first researcher to use them. In San Bruno, California, too, the Archives staff was most helpful in ferreting out documents that had relevance to my research, even though I had been unable to identify them in advance.

In San Francisco it was the staff in the Maritime Museum Library who referred me to the Bancroft Library at the University of California, Berkeley, where another treasure awaited me: 4 of the 115 cartons of the Kentfield Papers contained documents pertaining solely to the *Revere*. I am grateful for permission to reproduce some of the papers in this collection, which is particularly valuable since so few San Francisco documents from this period are still extant.

The G. W. Blunt White Library at Mystic Seaport possesses the captain's log of the *Revere*'s first voyage around the world, and I am grateful to the trustees of the library for their cooperation and for permission to quote and to reproduce some pages from this document.

I am indebted also to the late Leonard H. Dowse, great-grandson of Frederic Howes, for giving me access to the captain's logbooks describing his eight voyages with the *Revere*. It was a privilege and a pleasure to be allowed to peruse the manuscripts at leisure.

The Historical Society of Yarmouth Port, Massachusetts, has financial statements pertaining to three voyages of the *Revere*. I am grateful to the former curator, Mr. Hugh S. Clark, for extending his hospitality so that I could copy the materials there—in the kitchen of his home!

Just recently—thanks to the thoughtfulness of Captain Huycke—the record of yet another *Revere* voyage has come to my attention: Captain John D. Whidden's *Ocean Life in the Old Sailing Ship Days: From Forecastle to Quarterdeck*. I am now doubly indebted to Captain Huycke, whose Introduction to the *Voyages* provides a valuable and most welcome background sketch for this period in the history of American sail.

Finally, I thank my editor/publisher for his patience with my editorial convictions, for sharing his own expertise in maritime matters, and for all manner of guidance—from persuading me that some of the hard-gained minutiae pertaining to a single voyage are really expendable, to supplying bits of nautical background and detail that eluded me and, of equal importance, to alerting me to my unwitting land-lubber-isms [my word, unedited—not his!].

INTRODUCTION

The life expectancy, in general terms, of any wooden ship built before and after the turn of the century, 1900, was considered to be twenty years. That the ship *Revere* exceeded this rough actuarial milestone by another fourteen years is not extraordinary, though many wooden sailing ships of the mid-1800s struggled on into advanced age.

Fire, groundings, collision and heavy weather damage all took their toll of ships--as these assaults continue to do in the modern age on any type of hull--but the primary ailment of old wooden ships was, and is, rot. Rot was endemic to all. From the day of launching, the natural erosion of wood rot and metal wastage begins its relentless attack on ships. The *Revere*, which is the subject of Madeleine Rowse Gleason's interesting and valuable history, was no less exposed to these various attacks during her thirty-four year's existence. She had her share of damages and wear and tear, but continued a long and generally profitable career which spanned a significant era in American maritime history. In the end it wasn't rot which caused her demise. It was a fatal grounding.

Though the finer details of her construction are not preserved, one assumes that she was built of oak, fastened with trunnels and iron and bronze bolts and spikes, planked most likely with long leaf yellow pine, and was put together in the customary manner of the day, mostly by hand. Her decks were very likely constructed of white pine, caulked with oakum and payed with Stockholm tar.

Revere's fairly long life began in Medford, Massachusetts, at a time when the glorious and glamorous epic of the American Clipper was under way. Stimulated by the excitement of the China tea trade of the 1840s and the California Gold Rush of 1849, shipbuilders strove to gain days and weeks of ocean transit time by designing the famous hollow-bowed clipper ships. Like a streak of lightning in a passing storm, the clippers raced upon the scene, and stole the show, only to vanish within a decade or so. The Revere belonged to those times, but not in that class.

A study of her cargo manifests, passenger lists and documents, which happily have survived to provide the author with a detailed account of her voyages, clearly points to the fact that the Revere was a draft horse of the age, not a sprinter with the glories of record passages and fame. She was launched at a time when Matthew Fontaine Maury was well into, but still establishing, his reputation as an oceanographer and scientific recorder of ocean currents, weather and winds. With the results of Maury's studies, which established recommended seasonal routes for sailing ships in the North Atlantic and the world's oceans, Revere kept company in a more or less scheduled service carrying passengers and freight. The reliability of fixed dates for departures and arrivals was obviously flawed because of uncertainties of weather but it was a good try and the schedules of sailing ships worked to a satisfactory degree.

Transatlantic passengers were as likely to travel in ships such as the Revere as they were in steamers, although steamers were appearing on the Western Ocean routes, establishing schedules, and carrying mail and high-revenue freight. A look at the Revere's cargo manifests will illustrate that she was, at times, a floating hardware store and also carrying passengers in her cabins. Immigrants from North Europe are listed by the hundreds in the Revere's manifests.

Revere was a transitional type of ship. She set stunsails, light and oft-used sails of lightweight cotton duck which have been more dramatically associated with clippers and a much earlier breed of Navy warship. And she was originally built and rigged with single topsails. These features and this period in American shipbuilding history set the tone and help to fix the *Revere*'s position in that parade of ships. She is related to the Western Ocean packets of earlier times, and the larger Downeaster of the post-Civil War years. *Revere* was built in the year when California clippers and China clippers were being laid down in the Donald McKay yard of East Boston, as well as other yards in the vicinity of Medford, Connecticut and New York. A scant few miles away, Donald McKay launched the clipper *Reindeer* in the summer, while the *Revere* was still in frame, or being planked.

    Revere is a significant ship in one respect in that her first master was the inventor and patent-holder of the double tops'l. The painting of the ship which inspired the author's research clearly shows three reef bands across three deep single tops'ls, no doubt the original rig of the ship. Like anything new, the concept of introducing an innovative idea like an upper and lower tops'l, in lieu of a single, deep, labor-intensive sail, was refused by the principal owners of the ship. But Capt. Frederic Howes, the ship's first master, persisted in his effort to introduce this feature on the *Revere*, and indeed succeeded before he relinquished command to a successor, then taking command of a newer ship *Climax*. *Climax* is described as having double tops'ls almost from the beginning of her existence.

    Not only is the *Revere* credited with being the first ship with double tops'ls, but Capt. Howes applied for a patent for same and was granted this distinction and rights to royalties on 20 June 1854. The idea quickly caught on and the "Howes Rig" was adopted and installed on square riggers worldwide. Mr. Rob Napier cites at least one instance ("The American Neptune," Vol. 47, No. 2, Spring 1987) where Capt. Howes received a royalty payment of $78.70 for his invention installed on the newly-built *Sooloo* in 1861. How many honest payments he received thereafter during his lifetime from worldwide shipbuilders and ship-owners, one can only imagine.

    Revere is treated to further contemporary writings in which the grounding and bottom damage suffered at Tierra del Fuego in early 1854 is thoroughly described by Capt. John Whidden, who was at the time signed on as second mate. The travail of the master and the crew in dumping the ice cargo overboard and pumping a good quantity of the Atlantic Ocean through her seams and damaged planking is thoroughly described in Capt. Whidden's book "Ocean Life in the Old Sailing Ship Days" (Little, Brown and Co., Boston, 1908). Not many of the work horse tramping sailing ships of the mid-19th Century were written about to any extent. But *Revere* is an exception.

The storage and preservation of certain documents related to ships is the task of the National Archives. The complete inventory of a given ship's registries, enrollments, manifests and commercial papers is maintained in various archives around the American continent, and it is a repository of the essentials of any vessel's progress through life. Madeleine Rowse Gleason has dug deeply into this paper treasury and from its depths has drawn the records of the *Revere* and built the framework of her history, which takes the reader from the launching ways in Medford to the rocky beach off Port San Juan, Vancouver Island, where the *Revere* piled up.

The detail and thoroughness of the compilation of the manifests which the archives afforded the author, and the supplemental letters and private papers which were sought and found by the author, all make a very interesting mix of the business of operating the *Revere* during her fairly long career. Fortunately the National Archives have always been a repository for such records, and now as this ship's history is being preserved in book form, there are maritime museums being built and supported along the nation's coastlines which further preserve those family and obscure private documents which are yet being found in attics and trunks. The Pacific Coast collections were not organized or gathered together until the end of World War II. Now such good works as this one of Madeleine Rowse Gleason reopen those nearly closed doors which have been shut on the 19th Century's shipping scene.

Revere tramped across the Atlantic and Pacific Oceans and survived the Civil War at sea. Well clear of the immediate war zone, but not entirely free of risk from the Confederate raiders in the Pacific, *Re-*

vere arrived in the Pacific Northwest, and loaded lumber at Port Gamble in 1864. Here was one of the earliest mills, built on Puget Sound by men from Boston and Maine who were attracted to the West by the gold fever, but were also lured by the new opportunities of business which the untapped timber riches of the Northwest afforded the venturesome spirit.

The Port Gamble mill, built and operated by the Puget Mill Company, had been in business for about eleven years when the *Revere* arrived in the Sound in 1864 to load a cargo of lumber. The loading required two months. Elapsed time for loading in those years was of less concern to owners than it was in the decades that followed. The *Revere* had no engines to consume oil and eat up part of the owner's revenue from the lumber cargo. The mill production was doubtless such that the ship waited for one load after another to come from the saws and sorting piles, one day following another, as the logs were bullied into the mill and cut into long lengths of rough-cut lumber. It was a primitive lumbering manufacturing plant, this Puget Mill Company operation, owned by the Popes and Talbots of Maine. At first the mill produced about 2,000 board feet a day, which would exceed only a modern saw mill straddle-carrier load by today's measurements. The mill's output had increased, especially with the demands for ships' spars in Britain and the U.S. East Coast, and the growth of San Francisco and California cities and of the export markets being developed around the Pacific Ocean, not the least of which was the commercial development of Hawaii.

Shipbuilding on the Pacific Coast began soon after the advent of the frantic Gold Rush. The first ships were small and used for local, river and coastwise traffic. With the development of the Northern California and Washington lumbering and milling industries, shipbuilding lagged insofar as the need for lumber-carrying vessels was concerned. Thus the lumber fleet which was formed by mill owners and shipowners consisted of second-hand Atlantic coast-built vessels, which had a history of hauling bulk cargoes, cotton, passengers and general cargo—but not lumber. They were not entirely suited for the lumber trade, but they served their owners well enough in the carriage of other commodities, notably coal, which was a deadweight cargo.

The physical characteristics of the Atlantic packet, such as *Revere*, had limitations for the efficient and relatively easy stowage of lumber. On deck, the web of rigging, including numerous backstays and shrouds, running gear and spars, made the loading of long lengths of lumber cumbersome and slow. These early packets had small hatches, another obstacle, through which long lengths of lumber or timbers had to be passed, vertically pointed through the hatch and then drifted fore and aft into the far reaches of the hold. The presence of a 'tween deck only complicated this loading procedure. Thus the labor intensive work of filling a cargo hold with lumber took days, weeks and even months, and as stated above, this was often governed by the daily or weekly output of the mill. Handling long timbers and planks, say 24' to 40' in length, was a tedious job.

The cutting of bow ports and stern ports above the deep load line facilitated the loading of long lengths of lumber into the lower holds. There were hazards in this, and not a few ships suffered dangerous leaking from careless or inadequate caulking and securing of the closed bow and stern ports when ready for sea. There is apparently no record that *Revere* was thus altered for her lumber cargoes, but she may have been.

Coal, on the other hand, was a bulk commodity loaded by some mechanical device, such as a chute, bucket or belt, and could be trimmed by hand to fill the hold and 'tween deck to the maximum cubic capacity. *Revere*, like many of the older square-riggers which came from the Atlantic Coast, had hauled coal before and was therefore well-suited for the growing coal trade out of British Columbia and Puget Sound.

These overaged and redundant vessels from the Atlantic and Cape Horn trade were getting iron-sick and loose as they passed into their second quarter century of service. Stories survive from the Pacific Northwest that loading lumber in a few of the old square riggers was extremely hazardous in at least one respect. Caulking and the old planking allowed the inevitable leaking, even as an old ship lay quietly alongside a mill dock. Longshoremen in the hold had to contend with this leaking, and on some rare occasions were obliged to swim to safety. On at least one occasion a longshoreman drowned in the rising flood while trying to load lumber in the hold.

Revere kept company with others of her generation from the New England shipyards, such as the bluff-bowed *Samoset*, built in Portsmouth, New Hampshire in 1847; the ship *Shirley* built in 1850, also in Medford, Massachusetts; the medium clipper *Dashing Wave*, built in 1853 in Portsmouth, N.H.; and the *David Hoadley*, a bark of 984 tons which was built as a ship in New York in 1854. The medium clipper *Blue Jacket II* dating from 1864 likewise found her last calling in the Pacific lumber and coal trades.

The settlements which took root along the Pacific Coast, north of San Francisco, were located near the few navigable harbors and barports, where ships could enter. Ocean-going ships had a hard time of it, trying to cross undredged breaking bars, or anchoring and mooring in semi-protected dog-holes of Northern California where the sawmills were being built. There were many losses of ships and lives. But the demand for shipping not only provided an extended life for the aging East Coast packets and clippers, but brought shipbuilders to the fir and redwood forests. Close by the mills which supplied the planking, simple slipways and sites were laid out and small schooners and early steamers were built for the local commerce.

An immigrant shipbuilder, Thomas Petersen, built the first two three-masted schooners in Northern California in 1866. The first four-masted schooner was built by Captain A. M. Simpson on North Bend, Coos Bay, Oregon in 1886. The first five-masted schooner *Louis* was likewise built in Coos Bay by John Kruse for Simpson in 1888.

Schooners and the popular barkentine in greater numbers were produced in numerous yards from San Francisco to Puget Sound, nearly all of which were built specifically for the lumber trade. As we have seen, lumber was not a deadweight cargo, which meant that the construction of the ship, its shape and arrangement, had to be such that the maximum quantity of lumber could be carried, not only below decks, but on deck. And the evolution of this new design of hull precluded the need for ballast altogether or limited it to small quantities. This was a distinct advantage which the new West Coast lumber ships had over the dead-weight carrying square-riggers brought from the Atlantic. A four-masted schooner with a full deckload, for example, could carry fully one-third of the cargo on deck, chained and lashed down to a height of perhaps twelve feet thus making the combination of cargo and ship one huge floating wood pile. As seaworthy vessels they were extremely safe.

Square-rigged ships, such as barks and full-rigged ships, were built in only a few places in the Pacific Northwest for a period of only twenty-one years. Eleven barks and three full-rigged ships were built between 1869 and 1890, which ships were employed in the Cape Horn grain trade, Pacific Coal trade, general cargo and the growing lumber trade. But it was the fore-and-after and the efficient barkentine which dominated the shipbuilding industry in the more than half century after 1850.

The builders came from Europe, Canada's maritime provinces and the New England states. They brought with them the skills and practices of the North Sea, Baltic and the North Atlantic, but what they found was an endless supply of Douglas fir trees from which were sawn the longest lengths of clear grain, shipbuilding-quality planking that did not exist in the old world. Competing with the East Coast builders, and those in Britain who were perforce turning to iron and then steel sailing ship construction, the West Coast builders had one distinct advantage. Labor was becoming plentiful, and the ease of establishing a shipbuilding site adjacent to a sawmill on tidewater made it a common practice.

Revere and her Atlantic Coast sisters inevitably faced redundancy as the passing of years and the newbuilding West Coasters entered the competition. The author describes the declining value of the *Revere* in the ship's last years, and one can only assume that the bluff-bowed old coal drogher, in her thirties, was being coppered, caulked and repaired at a greater cost to her owners, and in 1875 she was rigged down to a bark, thus reducing the size of the crew.

Stunsails were redundant in the Pacific and required a bigger crew than a four-masted schooner with only four or five men in the forecastle. What was the hurry? Lumber didn't spoil. As a coal carrying ship, *Revere* was now the servant of the trans-Pacific passenger steamers which stopped in Honolulu for coal bunkers. *Revere* continued hauling the black diamonds from British Columbia to Hawaii until the very end.

Finally it was a simple case of fog and perhaps bad luck which brought *Revere* into the Strait of Juan de Fuca in September 1883 and too close to the beach at Port San Juan (now known as Port Renfrew) almost directly across the Strait from Cape Flattery. Once hard aground and beyond salvage, the old ship caved in and fell apart.

The comprehensive history of the last half of the 1800s of Pacific Coast shipping history has not yet been written, despite numerous studies of lumber companies, commercial companies and individual men and ships. The track of the *Revere* is found here and this history of the former Atlantic packet is a very good testimony of the economics which attracted the ship to the Pacific Coast and the growth of the Pacific Northwest in particular.

Harold D. Huycke
7 February 1994

1

IN THE NORTH ATLANTIC
1849-1852

O sborn Howes was born with seafaring and trading in his blood. He developed his abilities quickly and soon became the epitome of the Yankee merchant. In 1828, at the age of twenty-two, he was engaged to act as both master and supercargo (a supernumerary in charge of trading and a critical position aboard ship before the advent of rapid communications) on a voyage to Brazil in which he purchased a quarter interest. The ship's cargo of flour, wine and cotton goods was valued at fourteen thousand dollars. Many voyages followed, on various ships in positions of increasing responsibility. In 1834, his was the first American vessel ever to visit Smyrna (now Izmir), Turkey, and was inspected with great interest by the Pasha. When his first wife died in 1836, Osborn Howes closed out his career as a seaman. Nevertheless, on 6 November, a year later, he was admitted to the prestigious Boston Marine Society, founded in 1742. Thus, when he and his brother-in-law, Nathan Crowell, set up their partnership as merchant traders in 1839, Osborn Howes already had more than ten years' experience as a merchant trader in Europe and South America and was a recognized ship's master of high reputation.

A period of rapid growth in New England trading followed the financial crash of 1837. For the remainder of the decade an average of almost fifteen hundred ships entered Boston annually from foreign ports—twice the number for the 1820s when Osborn Howes was at sea—and the average size of the vessels increased as well. Coastwise arrivals were growing in the same proportion,[1] and the fledgling enterprise first directed its activities to the American market.

Osborn Howes was already part-owner of one bark and had lost another in a West Indies hurricane. Now, for the firm of Howes & Crowell, he and Nathan Crowell began buying corn and flour in the South, to sell in Boston. Business flourished. Gradually they built up their own fleet, bought the brig *Josephine* and the bark *Kilby*, and in 1845 started building vessels for their own use: the ships *George Hallett, Newton, Kedron,* and, in 1849, the *Revere.* For that year the city of Boston assessed the firm $15,000 in city tax—up $3,000 from the previous year.

As commission merchants the partners were now becoming substantial shipping merchants, who filled orders only from other dealers, "importing or exporting as they directed and receiving as commission usually 2 or 2-1/2 per cent. on the value [of] all such transactions," whether or not they owned the cargo-carrying vessel. The shipping merchant, however, by definition "owned, in whole or in part, his own vessel and exported and imported his goods thereby."[2] Thus the partners had the double advantage of booking their own cargoes on their own ships and carrying cargoes for others at a standard commission.

When the *Revere* was launched, she was the largest ship in the Howes & Crowell fleet and their first to have been built at the Thatcher Magoun yard—one of ten such facilities in Medford—where all the Hayden & Cudworth vessels were built. Although fast, the new ship lacked the fineness of hull of the true clippers, an innovation yet a few years away. In November 1849 she was towed—or poled—the five miles down the Mystic River, and tied up at Commercial Wharf in Boston, with no master or destination announced.[3] Her first insurance policy, which lists the

This scene on the Mystic River is typical of the way the *Revere* was launched. **Charles Brooks,** *History of the Town of Medford, Middlesex County, Massachusetts*

vessel's value at $48,000, was issued on 8 December 1849 to commence at noon, with coverage for $1,000 for one year at six percent per annum. Two days later, her first permanent register was issued at Boston. It included not only the names of the owners, their places of residence, and the number of shares each owned, but also the description and admeasurement of the ship as prepared by the deputy surveyor for the District of the Port of Boston: "that the said Ship or Vessel has two Decks and three Masts and that her length is One Hundred, & fifty seven feet, her breadth Thirty one feet, nine & half inches, her depth Twenty two feet, nine inches, that she measures Seven hundred thirty four Tons 12/95ths, that she is a Ship, has a square stern, and a billet head."[4]

"Having been specially fortunate with our ships," Osborn Howes noted in his autobiography, "our friends at South Yarmouth were quite willing to join with us either in building or in purchasing such ships as was judged best, so that for many years the entire control of affairs was left to our discretion, and we generally acted without much consultation with the parties interested."[5]

Table 1. Owners and Shares in the Revere

Owner's name	Residence	1849	1853	1862	1863	1864	1865	1878	1882
Osborn Howes }	Boston								
Nathan Crowell }	"		11/32	13/32					
H. S. Hallett	"		4/32						
Eben Howes, Master	Duxbury		4/32	4/32					
George Lovell	Barnstable		2/32	2/32					
Isaiah Crowell	Yarmouth		4/32	4/32					
D. K. Akin	"		2/32	2/32					
Dan. Killey	"		2/32	2/32					
Silas Baker	"		1/32	1/32					
Nathan S. Simpkins	"		1/32	1/32					
Dan. Crocker	"		1/32	1/32					
Oliver Eldridge	Boston			2/32	1/16	1/16			
Ezra St. Baker	"				7/16	1/16	2/16		
Charles Merrill, Jr.	"				6/16	1/16	1/16		
B. Storey	"				2/16				
Laban Howes, Master	Dennis					16/64	16/64		
Josiah Nickerson	"					2/64	2/64		
Wm. Baker	"					1/64	1/64		
Wm. F. Howes	"					1/64	1/64		
David Lincoln	Brewster					4/64	4/64		
Geo. Mariner	New York City					4/64	2/64		
Nymphus C. Hall	"					1/64	1/64		
David Crowell	"					1/64	1/64		
Henry V. Schenck	"					8/64	1/64		
Howes Baker	"					1/64	8/64		
Alpheus H. Baker	"					1/64	1/64		
Levi Stephens }	San Francisco								
Colin C. Baker }	"					8/64	8/64		
Judah Baker, Jr. }	"								
Benjamin K. Hugh	Boston					1/16	1/16		
John Kentfield	San Francisco						1/3	1/3	1/3
Levi B. Mastick	"						1/3		
Calvin Paige	"						1/3	1/3	
E. E. Kentfield	"							1/3	1/3
J. McIntyre, Master	Pt. Townsend, W.T.								1/3

And so it must have been with the *Revere*. Of the thirty-two shares issued (table 1) the firm owned eleven; another eleven were divided among six of their Yarmouth friends and relations: Isaiah Crowell, gent.,[*] Nathan's father, an insurance broker, who issued the first policy on

---

[*] In legal documents "gent.," short for gentleman, was used to indicate a person who has no occupation (*Oxford English Dictionary*, s.v. "gentleman").

The first permanent register of the ship *Revere*, National Archives, RG 589

the *Revere* on 8 December 1849; David K. Akin, merchant, owner with Isaiah Crowell and David Kelley of an oil-cloth factory in Yarmouth, and a brother-in-law of both Osborn Howes and Nathan Crowell; Daniel Killey [Killea], gent., Akin's first cousin and likewise a brother-in-law of both Osborn and Nathan; Silas Baker, gent., another brother-in-law of both

No. *1490* **THIS POLICY OF INSURANCE WITNESSETH,**
That ISAIAH CROWELL & CO.

do by these Presents cause *Nathaniel S. Simpkins of Yarmouth* to be insured, lost or not lost, *one thousand dollars on the Ship Revere of Boston to, at, and from all ports and places to which she may proceed for one year commencing Dec' 8th 1849 at noon*

The *Revere*'s first insurance policy, Baker Library, Harvard Business School

partners; Nathaniel Stone Simpkins, a director of the First National Bank of Yarmouth; Daniel Crocker, merchant. The owners of the remaining ten shares were Henry S. Hallett, a Boston merchant; Captain Eben Howes, a former master of the ship *Kedron* and a brother of Master Frederic Howes; and George Lovell of Barnstable, a Boston merchant.[6]

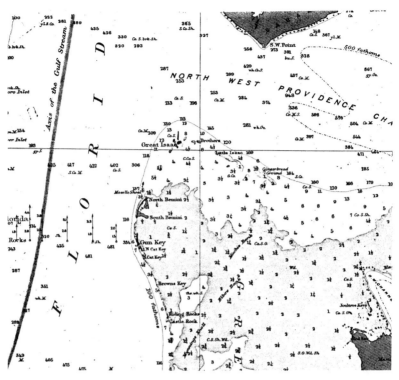

Chart of Little Isaac Island and vicinity. Courtesy, Map Collection, Harvard University

Her first master, Frederic Howes, was a native of Yarmouth on Cape Cod, like his employers, and like them a descendant of Thomas Howes, the progenitor of the family in America. He had been captain of other Howes & Crowell vessels: the *Kedron* when she was lost, and subsequently of the *Kilby,* for a single voyage. He would later achieve some fame in maritime circles as the inventor of the "Howes split topsail rig."*

Three days after the register was issued the *Revere* was cleared on a coastwise voyage for Tampa Bay and New Orleans, and shortly after noon on 13 December she made sail direct from the wharf, with a cargo

---

* *See* appendix A for an explanation of the "Howes split topsail rig."

of 139 tons of pressed hay designated for Fort Brooke, Florida, on government account.

Captain Howes' private log contains only routine entries of weather and sea conditions during the *Revere's* first week at sea. That would soon change as the ship's maiden voyage became fraught with difficulty. On 22 December, the Berry Islands, between Bimini and the Bahamas, were sighted. Then, at 2 A.M. on 23 December, the strong southerly current brought the vessel aground on Little Isaac Island. The crew immediately got out a stream anchor and kedges and went to work discharging ballast. The weather was fine and the captain "thought to get her off without damage." Ominously, several wreckers* gathered nearby, their boats drifting as they watched and waited. Twelve hours later the *Revere's* crew had unloaded only about seventy-five tons, and by mid-afternoon the next day the captain ordered the crew to discharge another forty tons of ballast. With a fresh breeze blowing from the northwest, they commenced heaving the ship again, and succeeded only in moving her

> astern about her length, and both hawsers parted; her stern swung around and took off a portion of her shoeing and caused her to leak . . . to the number of 1,500 strokes [of the pump] per hour. I had refused all assistance from the wreckers . . . as long as there was a chance for the ship's company to save her and get her off. At 8 A.M. [on Christmas Day] we then had been at work 54 hours night & day 54 hours and was completely exhausted, and was forced to receive the assistance from the wreckers to save the ship—which there was eleven sail collected around. At 8 A.M. I allowed them to come on board, but they would not do a thing to save the ship by the job [for] less than ten thousand dollars. So I allowed them to go to work to save her and take her to Nassau for repairs, which I thought at that time I should have to do; so they went to work discharging hay into their vessels.

---

* For centuries the Florida Keys and the Bahamas have been a graveyard for ships. During the last century many people made a substantial living by salvaging wrecked ships or assisting (for a predetermined price as in this case) ships in distress. When business was slow, wreckers were known to put out false beacons to lure ships aground. The profession was glorified in the movie "Reap the Wild Wind," with John Wayne.

Some sixty men were occupied in running out anchors and pumping the hold. Then, at 3 P.M., they tried heaving again—unsuccessfully—and put out about fifty tons of the cargo of hay. Twelve hours later they succeeded in getting her afloat in 3-1/2 fathoms of water.

At 8 A.M. commenced taking hay again, calculating to proceed to Nassau for repairs, . . . and I prevailed on the ship's company to proceed on the voyage if the [leak] grew no worse—giving my word that they should be recompensed for it to avoid enormous expense at Nassau. December 27 [26], 6 P.M.: Finished taking in the hay and securing

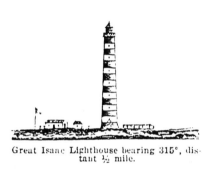

Great Isaac Lighthouse bearing 315°, distant ½ mile.

it below. At 7 A.M. some 25 divers went under the ship's bottom to see if they could find the leak, but could see not any part chafed except some of the shoeing gone & forefoot canted one side. 11 A.M.—I come to their enormous terms rather than go to Nassau to incur some $15,000. more and not benefit the ship any. We got under weigh and proceeded on our voyage at 12 noon.

Great Isaac Island was visible to the northwest, three leagues distant. At 5 P.M. on 27 December, off the Biminis, all the wreckers were discharged and the ship proceeded, with Gun Cay light soon visible three miles to the east. The next landmark was the Double Headed Shot Cays lighthouse at latitude 24.4 N, longitude 80.35 W, then Dry Tortugas, and

Double Headed Shot Cays Lighthouse

finally—on 31 December—the lighthouse at Egmont Key, just outside the entrance to Tampa Bay, where the *Revere* took on a pilot. On 2 January 1850, after dropping anchor some ten miles below Fort Brooke, Captain Howes proceeded up to the quartermaster's station to submit his report and get Major Donaldson's endorsement for receipt of the hay. "So ends this passage. 21 days from Boston"—and probably an eternity of twenty-five days from launch!

News of the December disaster was finally relayed from New Orleans by telegraph to Boston, and on 17 January the *Transcript* reported that a ship, presumably the *Revere*, was seen ashore on the Gingerbread Ground, "apparently but a short time on." The *Boston Shipping List* was better-informed: "New ship *Revere* . . . got ashore on the W part of the Gingerbread Ground, and was obliged to discharge into several wreckers before she could get off. They afterwards . . . rendered all necessary aid to the master, who settled their claim for salvage, by a draft on his owners, for $10,000, and proceeded on his voyage. The R was valued at $48,000, and is insured in this city for $46,500," which suggests that the thirty-two shares were worth $1,500 each, with Howes & Crowell invested to a total of $16,500.[7]

The issue of the government cargo, however, was only beginning. A charter party of 10 December 1849 provided for the purchase of the hay, which would become United States property as soon as it was paid for at Boston. Such was the understanding of both Nathaniel Winsor Jr., as government agent, and Howes & Crowell. The two partners subsequently preferred a claim against the United States, as owner of the hay, "for the proportion of general average assessed upon 139 tons of hay amounting to $426.94."[8] Common business practice required apportionment "of loss caused by <u>intentional</u> damage to ship, or sacrifice of cargo, etc., and of expense incurred, to secure the general safety of ship and cargo, in which case contribution is made by the owners, etc. in proportion to value of their respective interests."* The government officials in Boston, who had drawn up the contract, were of the opinion, however, that Howes & Crowell were to receive $24 per ton—double the market

---

* *See* appendix C.1 for a further explanation of general average.

price—to "supply, furnish, transport and deliver" the hay to Fort Brooke, and that the contractor was at risk until the hay was delivered.

By late April 1850 Howes & Crowell had received adjustment monies from their insurers in excess of $13,000: $3,731 from New England Mutual Marine Insurance Co., of which Osborn Howes was a director; $3,581 from Tremont Insurance; $2,686 from Boylston Fire & Marine Insurance Co.; and $2,984 from Neptune Insurance Co. The case dragged on, with Howes & Crowell re-submitting their claim in September and protesting that it was not the amount of money involved, which was insignificant, but the principle. In spite of their repeated argument that the government as owner should contribute to the general average, the opinion handed down on 17 October 1851 was that the Howes & Crowell claim should not be paid.[9] This apparently was based on the decision that the government did not own the cargo until it was delivered and was therefore not responsible to contribute in general average during the voyage.

The *Revere,* meanwhile, had continued her voyage. By 7 January 1850 four hundred bales of hay had been off-loaded at Tampa Bay into the steamboat *Berosset,* and the next day Captain Howes began loading wood as both ballast and cargo for the continuation of the voyage. He purchased fifty-four cords for this purpose and engaged men and a schooner to get it on board. Proceeding down the bay on the ninth, the *Revere* was aground for about two hours until the tide came up, so it was 10 January before she again passed Egmont lighthouse. On 13 January she "lay off & on all night," double-reefed, and the steam tug *Conqueror* towed her over the bar the following morning, when the tugboat *Phoenix* took her in tow to New Orleans, where she had only her ballast to declare.[10]

Clearing at New Orleans on 20 March, the *Revere* sailed for New York two days later, with a large cargo of cotton, lard and meats shipped by F. L. Dana of Boston as agent (table 2). Whereas the southward journey from Boston had taken thirty-four days, the passage to New York, without the attendant groundings, off- and on-loading of cargo and repairs, was accomplished in only thirteen. While still in Caribbean waters, she sighted several sail, but Howes reported triumphantly that his ship passed them all. The voyage continued without event until 31 March, when Captain Howes characterized it as "a chapter of accidents. We lost a man overboard, scalded the cook, and two suckling pigs got killed—a severe gale of wind during the 24 hours from N & W." She sighted land at 8 A.M. on 4 April, took on a pilot at 8:30 and came to anchor at noon, four miles outside the Sandy Hook, New Jersey, lighthouse. "So far, so good"—a favorite epilogue in Captain Howes' private logbook.

The newspapers were soon listing the *Revere* among the vessels from New York up for Liverpool, c/o Dunham & Dimon, commercial merchants at 67 South Street.[11] She cleared on 27 April with a cargo of 607 bales 4,918 bags of cotton, 30 dozen brooms and an unspecified tonnage of tar—all consigned to Pilkington & Wilson in Liverpool [voy-

Table 2. Voyage 1 cargo: New Orleans to New York

Product	Amount	Consignee
Cotton	972 bales as follows:	
	155 bales	Youngs, Hawkins
	185 bales	H. Colt
	377 bales	A. Averell & Co.
	60 "	W. J. King & Co.
	22 "	Holbrook & Nelson
	50 "	W. Grosvenor
	51 "	J. D. Burgess
	72 "	Wadsworth & Nelson
Beef	158 tierces	N. T. Hubbard
	... hhds [hogsheads].	
Ham	1,214 tierces	E. D. Morgan & Co.
	52 hhds.	
Ham	68 hhds.	N. T. Hubbard
Lard	658 tierces, 151 bbls.	N. T. Hubbard & Son
Lard	658 tierces, 151 bbls.	order
Lard	99 bbls.	Frost and Converse
Pork	1 shoulder, 1220 bbls.	N. T. Hubbard & Son

Source: New York Shipping and Commercial List, 24 Apr 1850.
Note: cargo consigned to "order" was for the account of the supercargo or captain.

age 2]. After presenting his ship's register, the crew list and articles, receipts for port charges and a bill of health, the master received permission to "sail foreign."[12]

In addition, articles of engagement were drawn up at Fulton Ferry, Brooklyn, listing the names of captain, mate and second mate, two carpenters, one steward, one cook, and fourteen seamen, with the rate of pay, age, and place of birth of each. It was a mixed crew, from points in the eastern United States ranging from Maine to Louisiana and from Scandinavia, and between twenty-one and forty-five years of age. The mate was to receive $35 per month, the steward $25, the carpenters $23 each, the cook $19, and the seamen $15 each or less.

The course, logged from latitude 40.48 N, longitude 69 W at noon on 30 April, was almost due east. Four days out they "spoke" the bark *Envoy* from Philadelphia, probably only with flags, though possibly by trumpet, and a week later passed through a fleet of eight sail. On 13 May, when Captain Howes tacked to keep clear of the island of Flores in the Azores, he sighted four more ships "in the same fix." Another contest was in the making, for on the seventeenth he counted three sail in company—and was beating them all. Fastnet lighthouse, the extreme southern point of Ireland, was sighted on 25 May, and the following morning the ship reached Liverpool with "5 sail in company, but the *Revere* is the fast nag." The voyage had taken twenty-seven days in all.

Following the Revolutionary War, regular packet-lines were established in the North, coastwise to southern ports, and to Liverpool as well. A packet-line was defined as "two or more vessels whose owners advertised sailings to designated ports, on schedules as regular as wind and weather permitted, and which depended for their profit on freight and passengers furnished by the public, rather than goods shipped on their owners account." The Black Ball Line was the earliest among them. In the next generation the Boston lines servicing Liverpool suffered because of the city's inability to furnish eastbound cargoes. Cotton was a cargo much in demand in England in the early 1840s and could be procured only in southern ports, and the detour required for loading meant a sacrifice of the packet's passenger business, which was essential to success.

With the establishment in 1839 of Cunard's North American Royal Mail Steam Packet Company, with Boston as its terminus, competition for passengers began building. The average run to Boston under steam took at first fifteen days, then thirteen and a half. With the average for sail westward nearer forty days, "the sufferings of the Irish immigrants who came to Boston in these . . . vessels were hardly inferior to those of the seventeenth-century Puritans who founded our first settlements."[13]

On 14 June 1850 Tapscott's American Emigration Office announced their first-class packets to New York: the *Revere* would sail under their house flag on 18 June. Free cabin passage was available to surgeons, and private rooms for families or "Persons who wish to be more select," on payment of a one-dollar deposit.[14] In fact, the *Revere* sailed for New York on 22 June with no passengers but rather a large cargo of general merchandise, mostly iron and steel goods and crates of earthenware (table 3).

When the American consul endorsed the outgoing crew list on 21 June, he noted that the captain had signed on four new sailors for the return voyage to replace the mate, William Garrick, who refused to board, and two seamen who had deserted.

The first fourteen days were uneventful; Captain Howes had the satisfaction of running away from the packet ship *Patrick Henry*, with which he had been in company on 6 July. On 8 July he spotted several fishermen at anchor on the Banks, and early the next morning spoke the ship *Amelia* before he "passed her like a Dam." The cod-fishing was good, but the weather was deteriorating. On the fifteenth he had spoken the *Guy Mannering,* and three days later, to Captain Howes' great relief, the captain of the *Concordia* "ascertained our position as I had been out of an observation for 5 days!!" He immediately tacked to the south. Thirty days at sea, he noted on 22 July, was "long enough for anybody," but it was another three days—and another leak sustained—before the *Revere* came to anchor close to Sandy Hook, New Jersey, outside New York harbor.

On 10 August the *Revere* was at an East River dock, listed for Miramichi, New Brunswick, c/o R. W. Trundy Co., and bound on her

Table 3. Voyage 2 cargo: Liverpool to New York

Product	Amount	Consignee
ale	2 casks	D. Pilkington
bar iron	1438 pieces, 138 bdls.	Huntington
cannel coal	70 tons	order, &c.
chains	3 casks, 28...	Merritt & Co.
earthenware	22 crates, 2 hhds	F. B. Williams
earthenware	52 crates	J. Mayer
earthenware	29 crates	W. A. Francis
earthenware	30 crates	J. M. B. Bogert
earthenware	87 pkgs	order, &c.
glue	5 casks	order, &c.
hides	4 casks	order, &c.
hoop iron	106 bdls	order, &c.
iron	75 bdls, 1 bar	E. Corning & Co.
iron	1019 bars, 120 bdls	G. W. Shields
iron tubes	260 bdls	T. Prosser & Co.
lead	760 pigs	Strachan & Scott
leather	8 bales	order, &c.
rod iron	65 bdls	J. M. Huntington
RR iron	936 bars	E. Corning & Co.
RR iron	961 bars	order, &c.
sheet iron	160 bdls	L. Van Wart
sheet iron	516 ditto	G. W. Shields
sheet iron	9 bundles	J. M. Huntington
sheet iron	380 bdls	order, &c.
steel	20 cases	W. Boyd
steel	12 cases	J. Cammell & Co.
tin plates	510 bxs	Phelps, Dodge & Co.
tin plates	500 bxs	order, &c.
tyre iron	160 dls	order, &c.
whiskey	1 cask	D. Pilkington
wool	13 bales	Chonteau, Merle & Sanford
woolen waste	50 bales	order, &c.
mdse	20 crates, 20 casks	L. van Hoffman & Co.
mdse	1 truss	Harnden & Co.
sundry pkgs mdse		order, &c.

Source: <u>New York Shipping and Commercial List</u>, 31 Jul 1850.

third voyage for Liverpool "and such other ports and places, as the said master may direct."[15] Her crew of twenty was young—all between twenty and thirty years of age—and included Americans from seven states, plus one native each of Finland and of France. At 3 P.M. on 17 August the steamboat *Active* towed her to sea, and she dropped the pilot at 7:30. On the twenty-third, having passed Cape Canso light, the ship anchored half-way through the Gut of Canso, in seven fathoms of water. Three days later she took on a pilot who worked her up the bar to an anchorage up-river, where all hands set to work discharging ballast, in order to make room for cargo. "All well so far."

Loading the 23,384 deals [boards, 3x9 inches, 12 feet long] consigned to Gilmour & Co. required nearly four weeks. Not until 22 September was the ship underway, passing between St. Paul Island and Cape Breton Island in Nova Scotia. She ran fifteen days to Liverpool, where she docked on 8 October. Though the departure date had been announced for 5 November, the tug *Dreadnought* finally towed the *Revere* out on the tenth. When she reached Holyhead, six ships were in sight bound down in the Irish Sea, but she led the "van"; eleven sail in sight two days later. Ten days out, a gale from the northwest "carried away spanker gaff and split fore topsail, hove to under main spanker & main topsails;" the strong gales and violent squalls continued. "Horrid Chance to get to the West."

Thanksgiving Day was squally, too, but at least there were no leaks. Then snow and hail, and no ships now in sight, though the *Manhattan* and the *Philadelphia*, both bound west from Liverpool, had been spotted earlier. "Hard, hard luck!!," after thirty-one days at sea. When a "strong top gallant breeze" sprang up on 14 December, the captain promptly "made use of it" and arrived at Boston's Quarantine on 17 December, after thirty-seven days at sea. The 229 steerage passengers were all laborers from Ireland,[16] crowded in along with a heavy cargo of general merchandise loaded in Liverpool (table 4).

Indictments were later lodged against Captain Howes for allegedly having beaten and wounded Charles Thornby and John Smith, members of the crew, "from malice, hatred and revenge, and without justifi-

Table 4. Voyage 3 cargo: Liverpool to Boston

Product	Amount	Consignee
anchors	2	G. B. Upton
anvils	24	B. Callender
cannel coal	130 tons	E. Train & Co.
chain cables	3	J. Nickerson
chain cables	7	Whiton, Train
chains	10	Thatcher, Fearing
chains	17 casks	Whiton, Train
chains	12	order
copper	92 cases	J. Bradlees
elephant teeth	25	F. Tudor
gelatine	3 casks	Elliott & Greig
grindstones	3	Naylor & Co.
iron	1582 bars, 328 bdls	Newell & Andrews
iron	111 blds	I. Washburn & Co.
iron	1100 plates	Curtis Bouve
iron	225 plates	W. E. Coffin
iron	386 bars	order
iron wire	160 bdls	C. Howard
leather	11 cases	W. B. Reynolds
nails	140 bags	W. B. Lang
paints	100 bxs	M. R. Fowler
potatoes	30 hampers	S. D. Bradford
steel	234 bdls	L. Bullard
tin plate	251 bxs	L. Bullard
tin plate	51 bxs	order
tusks/elephants teeth	106	J. H. Spring
mdse, &c.	bales & pkgs	order
sundry persons	229 steerage passengers	

Source: Boston Shipping List and Prices Current, 18 Dec 1850.

able cause." Upon his payment of twenty-five dollars for each case, the prosecution was closed.[17]

The *Revere* was cleared on the fourth voyage of her career for Liverpool by E. Train & Co. on 9 January 1851 and made sail the following day from Lewis Wharf with a crew of twenty-one.[18] Her cargo consisted of 30 bales of cotton, 175 packages of apples and 566 of saltpetre, plus other merchandise—undoubtedly some of the bacon, cheese, chairs, fustix, logwood, old metal, oil, pails, shoe-pegs, madders, tallow, and isinglass exported to Liverpool during that seven-day period. A week after passing Sable Island the ship was "foaming" along under two double-reefed topsails (still single topsails) and foresail, in hail, squalls, and heavy seas. She continued "on the Speeds" for a couple of days, having lost the stunsail boom to the strong gales. Finally, on 24 January, land—then Cape Clear and Tuskar, the Skerries and Liverpool.[19] She was fourteen days out from Boston.

To unload and load again required nearly a month. The *Revere* with Captain Howes was still being advertised by Train & Co. as "the only regular and established line sailing from Boston semi-monthly, and from Liverpool every week."

> These Ships are built in Boston expressly for the Trade, carry experienced Surgeons, are noted for punctuality and quick passages, and are fitted up in a superior manner, peculiarly adapted to the wants and comforts of Cabin, Second Cabin and Steerage Passengers, and for the speedy conveyance of Merchandise. Their average passage to Liverpool is about 17 days, and their elegantly furnished stateroom accommodations offer great inducements to cabin passengers, who prefer a sailing vessel.

It was Enoch Train, a Boston merchant in the South American and Baltic trades, who decided in 1843 that the city must have a line of Liverpool sailing packets. At a propitious moment he met Donald McKay of Newburyport, who was gaining a reputation as a master builder, and signed a contract for the first of many packets—the famous *Flying Cloud* among them. And the timing was good, for with the Irish famine of 1846 the pressures to emigrate skyrocketed. Altogether, the line owned or chartered at least twenty-four different ships. Train's advertisements touted their style, while spelling out their exclusions: "elegant and extensive accommodation, no ice or lime taken." He made arrangements with railroads here and in Europe for through rates, and also did a business

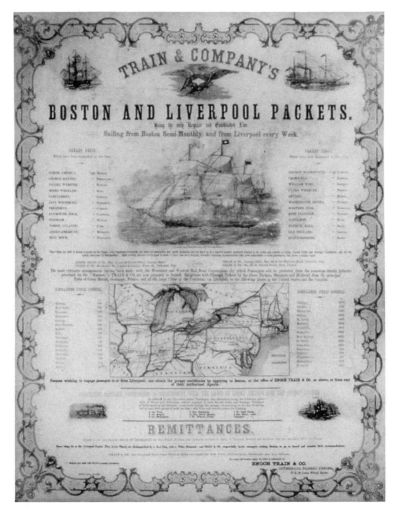

Enoch Train & Co.'s sailing card with the *Revere* listed fifth in the right hand column. Courtesy State Street Bank Historical Collections.

amounting to a million dollars a year, sending remittances from the immigrants to their homes in England.[20] And at Liverpool, where he competed with several other lines including Tapscott, he secured charters of nine sailings, transporting Mormon converts to Boston, New York and

New Orleans, between 1850 and 1857.[21] However, he had bad luck with some of his voyages, and by 1854 many of his ships would be under British ownership.

The sailing card gave addresses of Train's agents at Boston, Liverpool, and Cork. The agent could make arrangements with the Worcester and Western Corporation—"by which Passengers will be protected from the numerous frauds hitherto practised by the 'Runners'"—to furnish emigrants with through-tickets "from the principal Ports of Great Britain, Germany, France, and all the large Cities of the Continent" to points ranging from Nashville and New Orleans to Montreal, Ogdensburg, and Milwaukee. Also,

> in conformity with the laws of Great Britain and the United States . . . the following quantities of Water and Provisions will be supplied to each Second Cabin and Steerage Passenger *of twelve years of age and over* every week during the passage, commencing on the day of sailing, and at least *three quarts of water per day*; also Fires and suitable places for Cooking; 2 oz. Tea, 8 oz. Sugar, 8 oz. Molasses, 5 lbs. Oatmeal, 2-1/2 lbs. Navy Bread, 1 lb. Wheat Flour, 1 lb. Salt Pork, 2 lbs. Rice, and Vinegar.

No fare was named, however, nor was the estimated duration of the westbound passage mentioned.

The steam tug *Albert* towed the *Revere* out from the Liverpool docks on 24 February 1851. The first four days were comfortable enough, but soon the order was for double reefs again; the jib split (at latitude 48.10 N, longitude 36.30 W), and a stunsail too, so the voyage continued under three close-reefed topsails. Five icebergs loomed on 11 March, and ten more the following day. The ship passed through sheet ice that extended from northeast to southwest; the "sails all froze & Ropes so large that [the crew] could not haul them for reefing. Run with the yards on the Cap." Still, "so far so good!!!" at latitude 43.9 N, longitude 52 W, after eighteen days. On 14 March, from 10:30 to midnight, "a perfect hurricane from W.N.W. to N.N.W. it blew 3 double reef tops sails and courses to Smithereens!! Snow & Ice up to the Tops. Very cold so I run

PASSENGERS.

In the pkt ship Revere, from Liverpool, Messrs P S Stewart, of Canada; Andrew Hood, of Scotland; and 275 n the steerage, all well.

In the Undine, from Buenos Ayres, Capt Wm F Upton, late of brig Granite, of Salem, lost.

In the steamship Franklin, at New York from Havre, Capt J (perhaps Peter) Silver, of Salem, and 31 others.

her to the southwest for warm weather to get other sail bent." The storm lasted for six hours, after which all the split sails had to be replaced. The weather continued snowy and squally, but the twenty-eight day voyage ended safely at Boston's Quarantine on 24 March 1851.

The newspaper reported two passengers: Messrs. M. P. Stewart, of Canada, and Andrew Hood, of Scotland, in addition to 275 passengers in steerage, "all well," the same "sundry persons" who were mentioned among the cargo items (table 5), all laborers from Ireland.[22] Although one had in fact died at sea, the survival rate on this voyage was unusual, as was the speed: only seventy-two days to Liverpool and back.

This was hardly the touted average passage to Liverpool of "about 17 days." It was in fact the *Revere*'s second and last as a passenger-carrying packet. The steamers that now plied regularly between Liverpool and New York or Boston were faster and could offer more amenities than any sailing ship, with a greater return for their owners from larger numbers of rate-paying passengers. Steam was emerging as a serious threat to sail in the passenger trade—as was iron to wood—but as a dry cargo merchant vessel the *Revere* could still serve Howes & Crowell to good economic advantage.

On 8 April 1851 the *Revere* sailed in ballast from Lewis Wharf, Boston, for St. John, New Brunswick [voyage 5], again to load lumber for Liverpool. At noon the following day she sighted the Mt. Desert Island, Maine, lighthouse. On 10 April a pilot came on board off Grand Manan Island, and three hours later the *Revere* anchored outside, after a fifty-hour passage. On 25 April she cleared for Liverpool, laden with 19,888 deal ends [less than 6 feet in length] and 3 cords of lathwood, consigned to James & Morrow at $6,000.[23] During the loading there were thirteen desertions, and eleven replacements were shipped in St. John before the

Table 5. Voyage 4 cargo: Liverpool to Boston

Product	Amount	Consignee
anchors	4	E. Train & Co.
bar iron	207 bars, 600 bdls	order
cannel coal	50 tons	E. Train & Co.
chain cables	2	E. Train & Co.
chain cables	17	Howland, Hinckley
chains	8	E. Train & Co.
chains	6 casks	E. Train & Co.
chains	22	Thatcher, Fearing & Whiton
chains	7	J. Nickerson
chains	20 casks	order
copper sheathing	30 cases	E. Train & Co.
copper sheathing	38 cases	order
dyewood	11 casks	G. Searle & Co.
hoop iron	700 bdls	C. Howard
hoop iron	320 bdls	order
iron	2,564 brs, 100 bdls	Naylor & Co.
iron	2,662 brs, 120 bdls	Phillips & Mosely
iron	1,420 brs	J. Taggard
iron	771 brs, 459 bdls	order
mustard	3 hhds, 5 bbls, 12 cs	N. Snow
pig iron	50 tons	E. Train & Co.
plants	6 pkgs	J. J. Dixwell
salt	50 tons	E. Train & Co.
salted hides	10 casks	Spaulding & Bryant
salted hides	6 casks	T. Tremlett
sheet iron	352 bdls	order
sheet iron	200 bdls	order
steel	75 bdls	Naylor & Co.
steel	17 cases	Naylor & Co.
steel	6 cases, 125 bdls	L. Bullard
steel	10 cases, 5 bdls	Z. Hosmer
tin plate	300 boxes	S. May
tin plate	196 bxs	order
wheel tyres	36	Boston & Me. R. R.
wheel tyres	32	Taunton, New Bedford R.R.
wire	141 bdls	order
wire	10 cases, 95 bdls	Fullerton & Raymond
bales & pkgs mdse		sundry persons

Sources: <u>Boston Shipping List and Prices Current,</u> 26 Mar 1851; <u>Boston Evening Transcript,</u> 24 Mar 1851.

vessel sailed on 26 April. Eight days out, it was still "so far so good" for the master, and an uneventful arrival on 17 May.

When she was towed out the Mersey in ballast on 30 May, the *Revere* was "in company of some 200 sail.[!]" At Newport, Wales, she loaded 6,557 bars of railroad iron, consigned to W. F. Weld of Boston for delivery at New York. Having lost another seaman by desertion at Liverpool, she now shipped three more to make the full complement of twenty. On 26 June Captain Howes sent a letter by telegraphic twins to "Boquith" on board the ship *Zenobia* of Bath.* With five other sail in company, the *Revere* was in the lead, as usual. Howes could report, somewhat smugly, that one day later only one ship and one bark were in sight, "the rest astern." Strong gales finally blew in from the west on 12 July, necessitating "3 double reefed topsails and reefed courses. Large Sea. Ship behaves Beautifully!!"—but not for long. Calms and thick fog followed: "dull music to Have!!! Slat! Slat!" Finally, after twenty days at sea, a strong breeze from the west: "Tack & Tack. . . . What an outrageous chance to get to the Westward." When the breeze turned light, "they made all sail with the bar low," and made the Hook [Sandy Hook, New Jersey] on 4 August—after a forty-day passage.

St. John, New Brunswick, was the destination for her sixth voyage when the *Revere* was cleared at New York, in ballast, on 29 August 1851; "from there to Liverpool, and back to the final port of discharge in the U.S. . . . term of time not to exceed eight months" for the seventeen seamen, mate, second mate, steward, and cook.[24] Departure from New York was on 31 August, for a week's voyage to the St. John harbor anchorage. Even more desertions occurred than on the previous voyage, and sixteen replacements were signed before she finally sailed for Liverpool on 21 September. Deals and palings, in unspecified quantities, but valued at $6,285, made up the cargo consigned to Houghton & Smith. One week out, at latitude 41.38 N, longitude 51.15 W, the master "heard a horn

---

*The early semaphore code required the use of two flags, one in each hand, "moved to consecutive positions (indicating letters of the alphabet [or numerals]) as necessary to spell out the message." Good only for short distances, but very fast "in the hands of a highly skilled signaller." *Encyclopedia Britannica* (14th ed., [1939] and [1945]), s.v. "signal communication," "marine signalling."

blowing"—a distress signal, perhaps—but he failed to sight any vessel in trouble. On October 12—after twenty days, twelve hours—he anchored at Liverpool, where three more seamen deserted.[25]

It was to be the *Revere's* last voyage to Liverpool with Frederic Howes as master. When he returned to that city in 1855-56, as master of another ship, he was promoting the double topsail rig, which he had by then perfected. While staying in Liverpool he lodged in Mrs. Blodgett's rooming-house in Duke Street, along with Nathaniel Hawthorne, U.S. consul there from 1853 to 1857.[26]

The *Revere* cleared "with despatch" for New York on 25 November, as advertised, but ran into weather even before she reached the Skerries: a strong south wind carried away her fore topgallant mast. The entire voyage was marked by violent gales and snow squalls that required close-reefed topsails—even, at latitude 39.7 N, longitude 70.30 W, "a perfect tornado from NNW." The ship finally came to anchor off Sandy Hook on the day after Christmas and went on to 7 East River to discharge her cargo of general merchandise (table 6).

On 30 January 1852 clearance papers were issued for the *Revere* to sail on her seventh voyage, this time to New Orleans, apparently in ballast. Frederic Howes was still her master. She docked at Mobile, however, at noon on 19 February. Nine days out, she had anchored in a calm on the Bahama Banks (latitude 25.34 N, longitude 78.34 W) for more than twenty-four hours, perhaps thereby avoiding another disaster in the area of the Gingerbread Ground. After one of the captain's brief contests beyond Tortuga, he could happily record: "WE rather lead him." The cargo of 3,047 bales of cotton consigned to eight Boston merchants was cleared on 18 March,[27] and the *Revere* sailed out over the bar ahead of the *Charles Sprague.* Two days later, at latitude 24.20 N, longitude 83.30 W, the roles were reversed, with four ships in company, "all beating us shamefully." After two weeks at sea the ship ran into strong gales; the steering apparatus broke, and a jury rig of ropes and stocks had to be improvised (latitude 39 N, longitude 71.50 W). As Cape Cod came into view, four other sail were within speaking distance and the fishing was good. The *Revere* docked at Constitution Wharf on 9 April.

Table 6. Voyage 6 cargo: Liverpool to New York

Product	Amount	Consignee
anvils	2	G. Hoadly
bar iron	174 bdls	G. Hoadly
bottles	50 crates	Barclay & Livingston
colors	100 boxes	J. Macy
earthenware	57 crates, 1 cask	J. C. Jackson
earthenware	1 cask	D. Collamore
earthenware	14 crates, 5 hhds.	Vanbuysen & Charles
earthenware	11... 18 crates	J. Mayher
earthenware	8 crates, 10 casks	order
iron	989 bars	Cornett & Nightingale
iron	193 bars	G. Hoadly
linseed oil	6 pipes, 18 puncheons	Barclay & Livingston
mahogany	4 logs	J. Labone & Co.
mdse	22 bales	Francis Burritt
RR iron	1,350 bars	Vose, Perkins
RR iron	1,413 bars	order
salt pork	50 casks	"
skins	22 casks	Francis Burritt
skins	15 casks	order
tin	500 bxs	T. L. deWolff
tin	500 "	Barber & Pritchard
whiskey	6 puncheons	Cazet & Astoin
wine	57 cases	R. Makin
mdse, sundry pkgs.		

Source: New York Shipping & Commercial List, 31 Dec 1851.
Note: A number of other items are listed, but illegible. Among the other consignees were Brand, Cauldwell & Co., W. Chauncey & Co., Oelrichs & Co., and Phelps [Dodge] & Co. BDA (7 Jan 1852, p. 3, c. 3) lists iron, 1952 bars, 174 bdls; and tin; a total of 1775 bxs, but names no consignees.

A delay of several days in the harbor followed clearance for New Orleans on 17 April, with cargo, if any, in care of the master,[28] but she finally proceeded to sea on 23 April. The company, which included the *Mary Glover, Clarissa Currier,* and *Cordelia,* "made little speed. Not a very good chance when a person is in a great hurry!!!" Progress continued to be slow: east of St. Augustine after nine days at sea, and having passed the Hole in the Wall [the southern end of Abaco Island], the *Revere* entered the Great Bahama Banks on 7 May "in company with 10 sail, *Mary Glover* amongst them, which ship I hope to best." But the rival was soon out of sight ahead, though six other vessels remained in company. Dolphins abounded in the area, six of which were caught by the crew. On 18 May the *Revere* entered Mobile Bay with a pilot on board,[29] in company with the *Tam O'Shanter, Republic, Diadem* and *Robert Harding*. "So ends this fine passage of 25 days all West."

Captain Frederic Howes' imaginary contests with the many ships that came within his orbit were merely typical of the excitement that clippers aroused. In the course of the year 1852, "115 of them sailed for California, racing against each other and the time of the *Flying Cloud*." The demand for more and ever-faster clippers only intensified. They were driven "as hard as any had been driven before," and the sums wagered among builders and owners alike became astronomical. William Webb, the New York shipbuilder, wagered $10,000 that his masterpiece, the *Young America,* "could beat the *Sovereign of the Seas* in a run from New York to San Francisco." And, for his part, the owner of the *Sovereign*, built by Donald McKay, "advertised that he would return part of her freight money to shippers if [she] did not make a faster passage to Australia than any steamer."[30]

On 9 June, when the *Revere* sailed out in ballast, the *Charles Hamerton* and the *Empire Queen* were in company. For four days, in torrential rains, progress was slow. On the 18th, after Cuba was sighted, the captain tacked off of Havana, within five miles of the Morro Castle, and passed around the western end of the island. On the sixteenth day, having sailed safely over the tail end of Matanzas reef in twenty feet of water, he saw a grim reminder on the shore: a wreck, with nothing standing but the bowsprit (position: latitude 27.23 N, longitude 77.20 W). And on 8 July he noted "Cora's Birthday!!!"—the only personal reference in his entire journal—and continued to complain of the slow progress. At noon the next day Grand Turk Island was in view, and in mid-afternoon the ship came to anchor in New Orleans. "So ends this glorious passage of 31 days. Hoping our next will be better! High Diddle! Diddlety Dee."

Within a week 33,000 bushels of salt were stowed aboard, and on 17 July the *Revere* proceeded on the return passage.[31] The captain had little to communicate about this leg of the voyage other than his notations of the ship's position, the last of which read latitude 39.33 N, longitude 69.15 W on 28 July, east of Wilmington, Delaware. That is the final entry in Frederic Howes' personal log of his *Revere* voyages. He made no mention of docking at Battery Wharf in Boston on 30 July, or of the beginning of civil time, which he usually recorded.

One is tempted to conjecture that this may have been the moment when he tried out the new double topsail rig on which he had been working for several years. There is no evidence in his journal of any period when he sailed "forty-eight hours without any topsails bent," and on no other voyage was he so sparing of details. He later reported, however, that on one occasion, when the *Revere* was off Georges' Banks (about latitude 41 N, longitude 67 W), he had indeed "split two topsails and two courses, . . . I brought those sails into port just as they were, and requested my owners to adopt my rig on that ship at that time. They declined—had no faith in it. They said that perhaps when they built a new ship they might think of adopting it."[32] Whenever or wherever the trial may have occurred, a footnote to a biography of Osborn Howes by his son confirms the fact that the rig was indeed first applied to the *Revere*.[33]

> The double topsail, a device now [1894] in general use on square-rigged sailing vessels all over the world, was first applied to the ship *Revere*, Messrs. Howes & Crowell, giving to the inventor, Capt. Frederic Howes, who was then captain of the vessel, an opportunity to in this way prove the value of his invention. The use of double topsails has permitted of the carrying of smaller crews, and has also been the means of saving from destruction the lives of a large number of sailors.

As the first ship to carry such a device, the *Revere* achieved major historical significance in the maritime field. The reduced number of crew, of course, translated to less wages paid for the voyage -- an especially appealing prospect to a Yankee trader like Osborn Howes.

After the conclusion of this voyage Captain Howes turned his attention to the new ship that Howes & Crowell were having built at the Hayden & Cudworth yards in Medford. Having applied in person for a patent in "Washington City, D.C." in February 1853, he later bought shares in the *Climax* on which his rig was installed with the full approbation of his employers. From San Francisco, as master of the "ship *Climax* which has the rig," he reported at the end of July that the rig "is a great benefit. I can work her with ease 6 men less than I could with the old rig, and with more safety in heavy weather." The patent for the double topsail rig was issued on 20 June 1854, two months after the *Climax* had arrived at Hampton Roads with her cargo of guano. And it was only a year before captains sighting or "speaking" ships at sea were identifying the Howes rig from afar, even when they were unable to make out a ship's pennants or distinguishing marks.[34]

2

WESTWARD TO
SAN FRANCISCO AND
AROUND THE WORLD
1852-1853

With Captain Howes' transfer to the *Climax*, the initial, shakedown period for the *Revere* came to an end. Each of the eight voyages had been of less than four months' duration. As packet and cargo ship she sailed south as far as Turks Island in the Caribbean, north on the east coast to St. John and Miramichi, New Brunswick; still farther north, and east, to Liverpool, England, and Newport, Wales. Now, in mid-September 1852, after a short time at Battery Wharf and M Railway Wharf, we find her loading at Commercial Wharf, bound for San Francisco—the first leg of an around-the-world voyage destined to take thirteen months.

This voyage is unusual in the annals of Howes & Crowell because of the documentation that has survived: Captain Charles Hamilton's log for the entire voyage, as well as his meteorological reports and, for that first leg—fully as informative in their way, and far more interesting to read—the letters written by a passenger to San Francisco and soon published in the *Boston Cultivator*. A portion of the diary of that passen-

29

ger, John Swett, a young schoolteacher from Pittsfield, New Hampshire, has also survived.

Charles W. Hamilton, who returned from Calcutta as master of the ship *Singapore* only a month previously, was the new master. In Boston the commercial district was so well-peopled with suppliers of a variety of merchandise that "a merchant could make up at short notice, within half a mile of State Street, an export cargo containing the entire apparatus of civilized life, from cradles and teething-rings to coffins and tombstones."[1] Nathaniel Winsor, Jr., the shipping agent and father of the future historian Justin Winsor, had assembled a vast, mixed cargo to be shipped on the *Revere*—varied enough to appeal to the tastes and needs of New Englanders now transplanted to San Francisco, where the demand for flour, potatoes, lumber, and tools had soared, along with the freight rates for shipping.

When she sailed out of Boston harbor shortly after noon on 15 September 1852 on her ninth voyage, the *Revere* had on board, in addition to her crew and the assorted cargo, seven cabin passengers. Matthew Holmes Allen, of West Tisbury, Martha's Vineyard, and a native of Pittsfield, Massachusetts, booked passage with his wife and three children. John Swett, a native of Pittsfield, New Hampshire, and a former instructor at the Pembroke, New Hampshire, Military Academy, managed to accumulate the two hundred dollars passage-money each for himself and for his friend Joseph C. Morrill, also a teacher. The *Boston Cultivator* described Swett, who had been a contributor to its columns during the previous year under the name of "JACK," as a talented correspondent going to San Francisco to seek his fortune, though unfitted "by mind as well as body to rough it in so hard a struggle."[2]

Hard it was, but Swett had few illusions about the joys of life in the mines and no intention of making his life there, and he continued writing long essays for the *Cultivator* for the first two years after his arrival in California. He found a position as teacher in the Rincon grammar school in San Francisco and went on to become the first State Superintendent of Public Instruction, with several California schools named

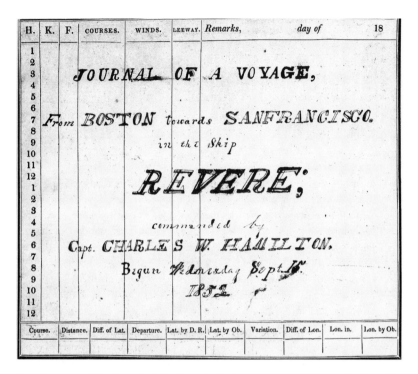

H.	K.	F.	COURSES.	WINDS.	LEEWAY.	Remarks,	day of	18

JOURNAL OF A VOYAGE,

From BOSTON towards SANFRANCISCO.

in the Ship

REVERE;

commanded by

Capt. CHARLES W. HAMILTON,

Begun Wednesday Sept. 15.

1852

Course.	Distance.	Diff. of Lat.	Departure.	Lat. by D. R.	Lat. by Ob.	Variation.	Diff. of Lon.	Lon. in.	Lon. by Ob.

Opening page of the journal of the *Revere*'s first voyage around the world. From the Manuscript Collection of Mystic Seaport Museum, Inc., Mystic, Connecticut. Used with permission.

for him, an author of articles and textbooks on education, and recipient of an honorary degree from Dartmouth College in 1878.[3]

Sailing day was "dull, drizzly, foggy and cold, with wind from the NNW." For all that, the ship covered 104 nautical miles by noon the following day. Swett later wrote that for the first month at sea the passengers talked with one another and read all the literature on board. Though there were occasional diversions, such as another ship close enough to be spoken somewhere southwest of the Azores, he observed that "time would pass heavily were it not for the companionship of books." On 10 October they were boarded by a boat from the whaleship *Philip DeLanoye* of Fairhaven, also bound to the Pacific, which stayed in their company for the next four days. On 19 October the *Revere* crossed the equator at

32.38 west longitude. Three days later, at 6 P.M., they sighted the northeast coast of Brazil and tacked to the east; saw a brig standing off shore, and a topsail schooner. But the young pioneer was finding shipboard life so dull that he resorted to reading Shakespeare and Scott and wrote long letters to the *Boston Cultivator*. The first of these is dated "At sea, off Cape St. Roque, October 24th, 1852."[4] They were then five miles off shore, and he noted

> a succession of rolling sand hills, covered with a thick growth of low bushes. We are four days from the equator, which we crossed in 32 deg. 30 min., but in consequence of unfavorable winds, have fallen so far to the westward that we shall be compelled to beat for a day or two to weather the Cape. A few small fishing "catamarans" are dotting the inlets of the coast, and by the aid of a glass we discover that the fishermen are in a state of nudity. I wish that one of them would come off and bring us the morning papers! But it is not probable that they have any papers in this benighted region; they do, in New England however, and to her rugged hills my thoughts have wandered while gazing on the sandy shores of South America!

He deplored the constantly changing weather and the feeling of ennui that pervaded the ship, referring to the

> unvarying monotony of our run to the line, where the fine pleasant weather was broken by copious showers, and the fair winds relieved by calms and squalls. A more unpleasant region than this same belt of equatorial calms cannot be imagined! The northeast and southeast trades meeting at the equator, a calm is the result, and the atmosphere being saturated with moisture, precipitates its surplus vapor in copious rains. The air is dense and close, and one can scarcely form an idea of its unpleasant effects. The lassitude which it imparts is unconquerable; it requires a great effort to read, thinking is out of the question, and the sight of pen and paper causes an involuntary shudder. The fear of sharks, which might prove rather unpleasant bathing-companions, alone prevents you from going overboard and splashing about in the deep green waters which look so deliciously cool. It is a great relief to feel the dry, bracing, invigorating air of the southeast trade-winds.

As they continued south-southwest, the captain noted a leak under the bowsprit when the ship pitched heavily, with the result that the pumps had to be manned most of the time. His log meticulously records courses, winds, currents, barometric pressure, position and distance at the end of each twenty-four period, with remarks on weather conditions, ships sighted, activities of the crew, and any unusual occurrences. The captain was also keeping a meteorological log for Lieutenant Matthew Fontaine Maury, superintendent of the Bureau of Charts and Instruments in Washington. Maury published his first *Charts and Sailing Directions* in 1847 and offered them free to the master of any merchant ship who would keep daily logs of "all observable facts relating to winds, currents, and other phenomena," in an effort to determine the shortest and fastest routes for the clippers to follow. No captains took up his offer in 1850, and only a few the following year.[5] Captain Hamilton, however, cooperated, providing Maury with a log at the conclusion of the voyage and made special notes of currents in his own log. The course was in general parallel to the east coast of South America. At about the latitude of the southern end of Brazil the ship ran into such strong gales and heavy seas that she pitched badly and took on large quantities of water, and the fore topsail split. The log records strong breezes, occasional rain squalls, and the same persistent leak—but the pumps were able to keep up with it.

After the Falkland Islands, more trouble: the fore topsail parted, breaking the parrel that fastened it to the mast, and then the outer jibs split. Now the pump was making at least 300 strokes per hour. On 22 November, for the first time since passing Cape Roque, they exchanged signals with two American vessels. Next day the captain wore ship to westward, in longitude 66.09 W. Cape Horn, or, as John Swett referred to it, "the terror of navigators, the mysterious region of storms and tempests, and the 'ultima thule' of the Western continent," was now fifteen miles to the north-northwest. Within sight of it, he wrote a long letter to the *Boston Cultivator*:[6]

> With an unusual degree of reluctance I crawled out of my warm, snug berth this cold morning and, buttoning up my coat, clambered up to the mast-head, as usual, to take a breath of the fresh air. I was very

agreeably surprised, and amply repaid for my chilled fingers and tin-
gling ears; for, in the blue line of the horizon clearly defined in the
morning light, I discovered a low, black line stretching away to the
south and terminating in a black speck, which I knew from our reckon-
ing must be Cape Horn! Fearing that I might be mistaken, and that after
all it would prove Cape "Fly-away," I remained straining my eyes until
the wintry blasts forced me to descend from the contemplation of the
sublime to the ridiculous, and renew my acquaintance with the choleric,
fiery, red-faced little fire-eater [stove] in the cabin, whom I found under
the care of the steward, glowing with a fervid zeal that would have put
to blush a New England reformer, or out-and-out abolitionist! We are
now within thirty miles of the Hermite Islands.*

The day is pleasant for these latitudes, the heavy swell which for
several days past rolled in mighty undulations from its southern home
has abated; the ship no longer plunges madly into the surges, bathing
her huge, black bows in clouds of snowy spray; she rides gracefully as
a drawing-room belle, spreading her broad white wings to the favoring
breeze! Another day and this breeze will take us past the islands scat-
tered around the Horn.

Nothing can be more desolate and dreary than the aspect of these
rocky islands, around which the ocean peals its solemn diapason. Many
of the mountain peaks are still capped with snow, though it is now mid-
summer; and by the aid of a glass, their seamed and rugged sides are
brought out in all their gloomy strength. There is something grand in
contemplating these grim old ocean mountains as they rear their hoary
heads into the heavens, resting their sunless bases in the unfathomable
depths of the sea—looking down on two broad oceans over which they
have for ages held their undisputed sway. Stern old sentinels are they,
lifting their shaggy sides from the dark waters that are dashing in thun-
der-tones against their mighty forms. . . .

Since losing sight of Cape St. Rogue, little has happened to break the
monotony of a sea-voyage; a sail in the distance, the capture of a
"booby," or Cape-pigeon, and the change from fair to head winds, have
served to interrupt, for an hour, the usual routine of our life, which is
eating, sleeping, walking decks and clambering about rigging for exer-
cise. Oh, for the power to sleep like Rip Van Winkle and awake at the
end of our voyage and find ourselves in the gold diggings. But why
should I wish it; I have more than six months work still undone. We

* Off the southeasternmost tip of Chile.

have been quite fortunate in encountering no heavy gales, though I earnestly wish for one, just to see the sea-king lead on his white plumed warriors of battle!

We are favored with numberless hail and snow storms which come howling and sweeping from the gorges of the rocky islands, and the mountain fastnesses of Tierra del Fuego. It makes the sailors grumble— this cold, wet, uncomfortable weather, and their bronzed countenances are getting as long as marlin-spikes. All human kind are grumblers, but a sailor is a grumbler par excellence. He is the ne plus ultra of the whole tribe of grumblers. It is perfectly astonishing what a list of anathemas and "sesquipedalia verba" he has in his grumbling dictionary. Place an old salt in the garden of Eden and he would growl because the apples of the tree of knowledge were not better!

Our ship is an excellent sea-boat, but if she chances to ship a light sea she is called by the grumblers of the watch "the wettest tub they were ever in"; the captain is a mild, pleasant man, but they growl about the "lazy old skipper"; the officers carry too much sail or not enough; if it is calm, we are to have a gale; if the breeze is fair, it is to cant round into a heavy wind. Every old salt solemnly avows his determination never to go to sea again; "a sailor's life is a dog's life"—this will be his last voyage; he only wishes to "get out of this bloody old ship"— all of which phrases are stereotyped, and have been repeated on every

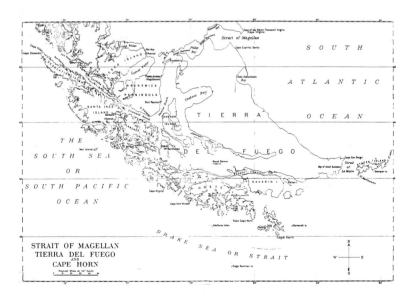

voyage, and on board every ship, for the last twenty years. Let them grumble! It is all the solace they have.

There is but little romance in a sailor's life off Cape Horn. It is nothing but "brace the yards;" make sail and shorten sail; shake out reefs and take in reefs, from morning to night. It is no pleasant duty to "stand watch" on the deck four long hours in a bitter cold night, when the sea air pierces to the bone, and old Neptune is treating his patients with a course of hydropathy that would put to flight a whole army of the followers of Presnitz, and then wet and shivering, turn into a cold bunk! I wish that some of the unfledged dabblers in literature who write such romantic sea-tales as appear in the "Star-Spangled Banner," "Yankee Privateer," *et in omne genus*, had to rough it before the mast round Cape Horn, they would then give sketches from nature and luxuriate over realities and facts.

I regret that I am unable to astonish you with marvellous accounts of "hair breadth escapes," and terrible gales, but we seem to be doomed to pass this great "bug-a-boo," in a very unromantic manner, not even getting a peep at the great white whale that has been cruising off here for the last thirty years, defying all the skill of the whalers, and laughing to scorn harpoons and lances, of which he must have, by this time, quite an assortment.

I will jot down a few items gleaned from various sources relative to Cape Horn and the adjacent islands. . . . Only the loftiest summits are covered with snow, for . . . the sea breezes melt the snows almost as soon as they fall. The mountains are covered with a thick growth of stunted wood and shrubs within a few hundred feet of their summits. . . . Their geological formation is greenstone . . . Fish are caught in abundance abreast of the rills of fresh water that glide down from the mountains into the sea. The natives . . . have a curious way of taking them; they tie a small limpet to the end of the line; the fish swallows it, and being unable to disgorge the living bait, are hauled to the surface of the water and taken into the canoe by hand, . . .

The natives . . . who roam over these islands, are certainly among the most degraded and wretched beings on the face of the globe. . . . Their countenances are brutal . . . they are . . . of small stature, and go almost naked in spite of the inclemency of the weather; . . . wearing a scanty clothing of greasy, filthy skins. . . . If the putrid body of a whale is driven ashore, they gorge themselves upon it. They are cannibals, and in the winter . . . they seize the oldest of the company, hold their heads over the fire till they are suffocated, and then greedily devour their own relatives and friends. Such is the testimony of a boy who was for some years a captive among them.

Having successfully negotiated Cape Horn, it must have been reassuring, in these vast expanses, to see two ships south of the Hermite Islands. Signals were exchanged with the *St. Peter* of Bath, and a boat from the English ship *Boadicea*, ninety days from Cardiff en route to San Juan, boarded the *Revere*. She continued in a southwesterly direction to latitude 59.20 S, longitude 74.23 W before changing her course more westerly. After 28 November, now sailing in a more northwesterly direction, two ships were sighted, bound east. On 7 December the captain found one of the larboard yardarms badly sprung. They were now in an area of fine weather and moderate winds, with a bark in company—at least for one day. December 24, sea-time, marked the one hundredth day out—"all hands on deck." Trade winds were moderate to strong; the fine weather held; the ship was tight, the crew employed as required, and they covered as much as 191 miles on the day that had begun at noon sea-time on Christmas Day. At 6 A.M. on 3 January 1853 they crossed the equator at longitude 109.30 W, about due south of the southern tip of Baja California, still heading north-northwest.

John Swett's next letter, which appeared in two installments in the *Cultivator*, takes up the story on 15 January 1853 in the North Pacific, at latitude 23 N, longitude 124 W, just south of the Tropic of Cancer:[7]

> We have had no rough weather in the Pacific; the royals have not been taken in since we were fairly clear of the Cape; we have had no calms yet; the breezes have been light and the sea smooth; for days together the ocean has seemed like some mountain lake ruffled by the free air of the Granite Hills; and over this ocean of tranquillity we have floated along, until lost in dreams of quiet beauty, life seemed more like a dream than a reality. What cared we for the busy, restless, noisy, exciting world, we were living in a world of our own—a world of romance, of beauty, of quiet pleasure. I have dreamed the old year out and the new year in, and would gladly dream away many more months; but a few days will close the pleasant voyage, and I must fulfil my promise of writing a line home.

I said that, since losing sight of the grim old ocean monarch that guards Cape Horn, the weather has been fine. We crossed the line on the 3d of January, at 6 o'clock, a.m., and the southeast trades took us into 4 deg. north latitude. After two days of light winds in the "variables," the northeast trades struck us; and, as if the breezes which had swept over the mountains of the gold land gave the ship a stronger heart, she sprung upon her course with renewed strength and walked away at the rate of 8 knots. The weather was remarkably cool in the tropical cloud region, at no time was it uncomfortably hot and we had only a few showers. The sky is now beginning to grow cloudy, the air cool, and the short days remind us of winter in New England.

We have been four months out, but have not yet experienced any heavy weather, and I fear that we shall reach port without witnessing the grandeur of an ocean storm. I have seen lightning but once, and have not heard a single peal of thunder. . . . Going out to California, as a passenger, round Cape Horn, is nothing but a pleasure trip, and working one's passage would not, by any means, be a terrible thing. . . . On board a ship crowded with one or two hundred passengers, there would be many things more unpleasant than in our present situation; for we have ample room, and the old *Revere* is a fine ship.

Her master, Capt. Hamilton, a perfect specimen of a live Yankee, Cape Cod sailor, is as pleasant and agreeable as the Pacific sea over which we are sailing, and it is but doing him justice to say that he has done everything in his power to make the passage pleasant and comfortable. It does one's soul good, in the present age of selfishness, to meet with a man who does not think himself the only being in existence. I can only say that the treatment I have received has been, in every respect, all that could be asked, and much better than I could expect, which, grumbler that I am, is saying considerable.

We are hoping to reach San Francisco before the close of the month. I said we, I should have said the rest of the company, for I am so well pleased with the life that I would willingly dream away another month on the Pacific. A thousand things crowd into the last days of a sea-voyage, as into the close of everything else. Passengers now begin to grow communicative; little animosities and bickerings and dislikes are forgotten, countenances that were absolutely unpleasant from looking at them so much begin to look friendly, and one wonders why he had any but kind feelings. A ship is a little world in itself. Its inmates constitute a miniature society. I believe it would be impossible for the best friends in the world to go a four-months' voyage and never have any falling out, or at least any hard feelings. The crew is composed of a noble set of boys, but now they begin to growl about small pay, sailor's life, old mahogany and chips, and to talk large of ten dollars a day and roast beef, a life in the diggings, and a fortune in a year. Why shouldn't they?

At nautical mile 15,039 from Boston, the captain's log of 16 January reveals no surprises. The *Revere* was now sailing a more easterly course, with San Francisco estimated to be 765 miles NE-½-E, and on 25 January only 468 miles distant. They spoke the bark *Fredonia*, 195 days from Cardiff en route to San Francisco; and on 26/27 January, with three sail in sight, they made the landfall that was identified as Point Baree de Arena [Point Arena, north of San Francisco]. Then the wait-

Journal entry of the *Revere* for January 16, 1853. From the Manuscript Collection of Mystic Seaport Museum, Inc., Mystic, Connecticut. Used with permission.

ing—strong breezes, cloudy weather, rain squalls, and fog for three days, "black as Egypt." On Friday, 27 January, the captain's observation read: "16,626 miles (one hundred & thirty five days from Boston); 2,275 miles less than I did in the bark *Morgan Dix* 1850." Next day they were off Point Reyes, twenty miles from the Golden Gate, with the weather clear and calm. They spoke a schooner that relayed the news that "Daniel Webster had died on 14 October and Franklin Pierce was president."

By 29 January, John Swett was revelling in the prospect of soon being at his destination.[8]

It is a glorious day. The sun rose up this morning, not from an ocean bed, but from behind the eastern hills, with a bright face, as if laughing at our ship becalmed, or rather smiling a welcome to El Dorado. It was a true *auriferous* sunrise; the hills were gold, the sky seemed gold, and the ocean below caught the reflection and turned of a yellow hue! My pulse thrilled with strange delight as I gazed this morning on the snow-capped mountain-peaks in the distance, rising grandly up through the clouds of mist!

We made the land on the 26th, Point Baree de Arena, a degree or more north of San Francisco, and since then have been drifting and beating about in the fog and rain, or lying "humbugged" in a calm! A calm in sight of a port is a most provoking thing to a sailor. Night before last was as dark as darkness could be, and the rain poured down in torrents, giving us premonitory touches of the "rainy season" on shore.

The cry of "Land-ho" is a joyful sound after a four-months' passage, and it falls strangely on the ear. I said the sun rose clear this morning— at the time there was only a little narrow belt of clear sky in the eastern horizon, but the clouds overhead were driven off into the Pacific, and now it seems a summer day. The ship lay all this forenoon like a log on the water, the current setting her off the land; faces began to lengthen, the old salts to *grumble*, the weather-wise to prophesy, and I began to *write*; but at noon a light breeze sprung up, and now (4 p.m.) with studden sails set we are slowly sweeping past Point Reyes, 20 miles distant from the Golden Gate. Point Reyes is a prominent headland rising abruptly from the ocean; we can see the surf dashing up the rocks as the long heavy swell of the Pacific breaks upon them, and can hear the low thunders of the breakers. Bearing nearly S.E. are the three clusters of Terra Lones [Farallons], naked rocks, looking like haystacks floating on the water. Near us lies an old schooner, jogging along as if loose in every joint, and far to seaward a large barque that we saw two days ago is bearing down.

Everybody is in a terrible hurry about nothing; the example is contagious, and I am wielding my pen in a hurry, though I have nothing to say. I am not half so glad to see land as I was to lose sight of it when we were "tugged" out of Boston Harbor! I feel perfectly contented here, for I know very well I shall find but few such easy berths. Willingly I would dream away another five months' passage. I feel just about the same reluctance to mingle in the scenes of active life as one feels on a cold winter morning, when forced to leave a pair of warm blankets and break up morning reveries; but were it not for action and excitement, what would life be! The crew have been busily at work for a week past; everything above decks is cleared up, and the old ship has put on her best "rig" to enter the port and greet her sister ships that are there congregated from all parts of the world. For my own part, I have formed quite an attachment for the ship, and shall leave her with many regrets—but the best of friends must part! If she could speak she might name many faults in me, but I have none to charge against her! Eight bells! "Please, sir, to leave the table," says the steward. I will leave it and you too—so for the present adieu.

On 30 January the *Revere* was still off Point Reyes, eliciting from Swett a new complaint: "Another Sabbath on the ocean!" But at six o'clock the pilot stepped on board "with a whole file of newspapers," which were of course an indispensable source of shipping news for masters of arriving vessels, as well as for owners and consignees. In its "Shipping Intelligence" columns, which included "Importations" and "Memoranda," the *Daily Alta California* published a list of vessels "spoken" by the *Revere*—complete with date and location—noting also that she had fallen in with the wreck of the ship *Pennel*, "coal loaded and abandoned"—which might well have been news to an unsuspecting owner.

Next morning, under a strong westerly wind, they "shot in past the Fort with an eight-knot breeze," and anchored opposite the barracks.[9] John Swett viewed the busy harbor:

Between us and the town sleeps a fleet of shipping; a large steamer— the *Pacific,* of Vanderbilt's line—is just going out of the harbor, crowded with passengers, miners with pockets and hopes filled with dust. Yesterday was a great day for arrivals, more than thirty sail of vessels entered the "Golden Gate!" I should judge that there were three hundred ships and barques in port; the masts form a forest. My state-room window opens to the southwest; as I write and I can see Signal-hill, on top of which is an observatory. When I awoke this morning and listened to the crowing of cocks, as the sound came down from the hill, I was fairly lost, and really imagined myself in a corner of the block farmhouse where I was born! I am ready to go ashore; the boat is ready too, and in half an hour I shall stand once more upon terra firma!

Devoid of passengers, the *Revere* shifted to San Francisco's California Wharf on 1 February. Collins, Cushman & Co. notified their consignees that she would commence discharging that very day (table 7); all freight charges must be paid, and "all goods remaining on the wharf after 4 o'clock P.M. must be stored at the risk and expense of the owners or consignees thereof."

The volume of imports from the East to San Francisco—provisions and grain, clothing and all manner of necessities for house and home—reached a peak in the year 1853, but by late 1854 the area was growing more self-sufficient. John Swett, who had gained a California-eye view of cargoes such as the *Revere* had shipped to San Francisco, observed that "the markets are still heavy, on account of the surplus of everything here. It would be well, if New York and Boston merchants would keep a little of their rancid ham and musty flour for home-consumption! Such things would sell once, but they can't be palmed off now! Many articles sell at wholesale for less than they cost in New York!"[10]

Once ashore, Swett described the city with boundless enthusiasm:[11]

The pleasant weather of the past ten days has dried up the mud, and the streets are in good condition. It is rather a curious sensation to walk the streets of a great city, feeling that you are a perfect stranger to every soul it contains, and that among the thousand countenances there is not a familiar one. I walked as fast as a thousand objects of attraction would let me, to the Post Office near the plaza, and was not at all

Table 7. Voyage 9 cargo: Boston to San Francisco

Product	Amount
agricultural tools	20 bdls
ale	50 bbls
axe handles	214 doz.
bags	13 bales
bedding	1 ck
boots and shoes	124 cs
boxes	50 nests
brandy	28 cks, 5 hf pipes
candles	189 cs
carriage	1
chairs	42 bxs
cheese	23 cs
chocolate	11 cs
cider	50 kegs
cigars	2 cs
clothing	41 bxs 27 cs 1 trunk
coal	263 tons
crockery	7 crates
currants	2 cks
domestics	170 bales
doors	1011
dried apples	13 hf bbls.
drills	17 pkgs
drugs	11 bxs
dry goods	44 cs.
duck	5 bxs, 100 bolts, 26 pcs, 2 bles
eggs	21 cs
fish	5 cks
flour	1887 bbls
fruit	50 cs
furniture	27 pkgs, 1 case, 93 bxs
gin	20 hf pipes
glass	4 bxs
groceries	13 bxs
gunny bags	230
ham	18 tcs
hardware	3 bxs, 17 cks 14 pkgs
hooks	27 pkgs, 9 cks
iron	45 sheets

(continued on next page)

Table 7. (Continued)

Product	Amount
iron hoops	3
lard	30 bxs 25 cs
leather	1 ck 50 sides
liquors	23 cs 100 bxs 112 kegs
lumber	60,000
machinery	22 pkgs
mackerel	200 kits 65 hf bbls
meal	225 hf bbls
molasses	41 kegs
nails	450 kegs, 300 bu. 631 sks
oats	1,501 bags, 300 bu., 631 sks
oats	101 bbls
oil	25 bxs
pails	50 doz
paint mill	1
paints	12 cs
paper	105 bdls 8 cs
paper bargings	15 cs
peaches	10 cs
peas	10 hf bbls
pickles	83 bxs 90 kegs
plough stuff	33 bxs
plough stuff	33 pkgs
pork	30 hf bbls
pork	400 bbls
preserves	87 bxs
preserves	4 bxs
rice	10 bbls
rope	37 pkgs 8 bales
rye	6 hf bbls, 150 bu.
salt	40 cs 25 bxs
sash	88 bdls
sheet iron	93 bdls
sheet iron	45 sheets
shingles	126 bdls
shot	13 kegs
shovels	126 doz 73 bdls
soap	100 boxes
spices	90 bxs
spirits turpentine	21 bxs
starch	100 bxs

(continued on next page)

Table 7. (Continued)

Product	Amount
sugar	322 bbls
sundries	1 bx 1 bbl
syrup	220 kegs
tinware	1 box
tobacco	40 cs 25 bxs
tongues and sounds	50 kits
tubs	50 nests 28 bdls
valeratus	50 bxs
vinegar	10 bbls 10 hf bbl
wagon stuff	160 pkgs
wagons	2
wheels	20
whips	1 bx
whiskey	25 bbls
whiskey	6 hf pipes, 23 8th cks, 59 qrt
white lead	4 half bbls.
windows	45 pkgs
woodenware	2 pkgs.
"do"	49 pkgs

Source: Daily Alta California, 1 Feb 1853.

disappointed in not finding any letters, for I well know that when a poor fellow goes to California, few think about him; he enters into a world of forgetfulness! Yet, after loading down the mailsteamer of yesterday with letters home, it was a little provoking!

The sight of the hills surrounding the city awakened all my old love for climbing mountains; accordingly, I started for Telegraph Hill. . . . The view of the city from thence is beautiful beyond comparison! The hill completely overlooks it, and the eye can take in everything at a glance! San Francisco is destined to be one of the finest cities in the world. On another hill, I suddenly came upon a gallows; certainly very expressive of the state of society!

The day is like a June morning; the air seems clear as crystal; the grass is springing up on the hills, a few little delicate flowers are opening their eyes to the warm sunlight, and everything is full of life and beauty! In the mere pleasure of animal existence I stretched myself on the green turf and drank in the magnificence of the day!

My notes of this city must be brief, though I should like to write pages, for there are a thousand things new and strange of which I could speak. It is hard to realize that this great city, so full of business, life and excitement, has, in spite of destructive fires, sprung up in the space of five years! There are many brick buildings now finished and many more constructing, giving the place quite a Boston air.

The large building in which Adams & Co. have their offices is a fine edifice built of Granite, worked in China by the Chinese. The markets are large and well supplied with all kinds of provisions, particularly vegetables, which are very fine. The potatoes are of a size that would delight the eyes of an Irishman, often weighing from five to eight pounds, and the cabbages would astonish old Rip Van Winkle, could he wake up in a California market. Milk is only five bits—a dollar and a quarter per quart, and potatoes only ten cents a pound! Flour, which was selling at $35 per barrel when we arrived four days ago, is now down to fifteen, and flour, to arrive, is sold at eleven!

The fine weather of late has made the roads passable, and large quantities of goods are going up in the mines. The surplus idle population of the city is floating away too, and business will soon become brisk.—The gambling saloons are still open and crowded with people every evening, but the rich harvests that they reaped in 1849 can no longer be gleaned; the gaming is on a small scale. Those saloons are fine places to study human character—human nature in its worst phases. In these haunts of vice, crowded with the depraved and dissolute, *women* are found, raking in piles of gold! Women, did I say?—they are not women, for every womanly trait has left them—they wear the form, but alas, how fallen!

Public opinion, that great leveler and irresistible engine, no longer favors these hells, and they are languishing, but there are hundreds of houses in this city still worse than these places, which to pass in the streets make one sick at heart, and from which one turns in disgust! Let the veil of silence cover them, they make humanity shudder! Strange that man will degrade himself below the level of the lowest brute— strange that, forgetful of his exalted nature, he seeks for pleasure in the cesspool of sensuality! Hundreds of Chinese women throng the city; they are Tartars, from the lower classes in their own country, and of the lowest here. There are sections of the city that can be compared only to the Five Points in New York! But I will turn to more pleasant topics.

There are eleven churches in the city, and many of them are well attended, but from the <u>mobile</u> character of the population, they do not keep pace with the growth of the city.

The public schools are in a flourishing state, though in consequence of great fires and heavy expenses no schoolhouses have been erected; schools are held in buildings hired for the purpose. I find from an examination of the records in the office of the superintendent of the city schools that there are six free public schools, attended by more than eight hundred children. These children come from twenty-seven of the states, from the Canadas, South America, England, Ireland, Scotland, Wales, Norway, France, Germany and the Pacific Islands.

There are in the city 1825 children between the ages of 4 and 13. For the year ending Nov. 1852 the city expended for schools $30,000. Before another year a system of schools, primary, grammar and high schools, based upon those of New York and Boston, will be formed, as movements have already been made for that purpose. The superintendent in his report says, "We may safely challenge all history to furnish a parallel to the high position which our public schools now occupy, in any city so young in years!"

If common schools are regarded with favor in the older states, much more important are they here as a means of elevating, assimilating and Americanizing the incongruous, heterogeneous and antagonistic elements that are brought under their influence. The private schools are numerous and excellent. Californians *live* fast, and they must therefore be educated fast and will soon take the lead in schools, as in business.

Five papers are published, viz:—The Daily Whig, Alta California, Herald, Times, and Transcript; the last three have a morning and evening edition. Besides these, there are four weekly papers—the Evening Journal, Golden Era, Christian Advocate and Pacific.

I might deal farther in statistics, but they are dry things, and I forbear. You can look for them in the Almanac. I only jot down a few things as they strike me, and you must pardon my egotism.

I am much pleased with the city and its inhabitants. The people are uniformly kind and obliging and willing to give a stranger any information in their power. All nations are represented here, but the prevailing and absorbing influence is New England. The restless, go-ahead, driving, bustling character of the Yankee is stamped on everything. There is probably no city in the world with the same population where so much business is done as in this. It seems more a dream of the

imagination than a reality! One can take up the Arabian Nights Enter-
tainments and deem it quite commonplace.

I leave for the mines tomorrow. The up-river steamers are laden
with freight and crowded with passengers daily, so for the present adieu.

The passengers were on their own. John Swett stayed with the
ship for a few days until he found a hospitable New England family that
would care for his possessions when he took off for the gold fields.
Joseph Morrill stayed in the city, where he later became principal of the
Spring Street school in the Vallejo district. He resigned in 1861 to serve
with California Company O in the Civil War, and became post-adjutant
at Fort Bragg; by 1865 he had risen to the rank of captain, and after the
war was superintendent of the Industrial School for wayward boys, just
south of the city.[12] As for the Allen family, they were not in San Francisco long enough to be included in any city directory, and there is no
clue as to their whereabouts after they left the *Revere*.

More than three weeks of work was in prospect for officers and
crew: discharging cargo and coal; taking on water, ballast, and supplies;
shipping men to replace those who had deserted. Finally, on 24 February
1853, the crew was complete, and a cargo of $5,500 worth of gold and
silver coins loaded on for Manila, with 275 tons of ballast. The *Revere*
was again ready for sea, drawing 12 feet 9 inches aft, 12 feet 3 inches
forward. Shortly after noon on 25 February the pilot took her out and
was discharged at 3 P.M. Three hours later the captain sighted the Farallon
Islands, east by north, his official point of departure for Manila. For this
era it had been a very short stay with a minimal loss of crew.

The course would carry them in a northwesterly direction for the
first two days, then southwest and into the trade winds—apparently with
fine weather most of the time, for the men were employed painting and,
in logbook vernacular, "as otherwise required." They passed to the west
of the Marianas, south of Balintang and across the northern tip of the
Philippines, in sight of Babuyan, and then Calayan, twenty miles distant;
past Dalupiri, Point Culili, and ten miles west of Cape Bolina, Luzon. On
11 April, after a passage of forty-five days, they were working short tacks
up to the Corregidor.[13]

At Manila extra hands were hired for discharging ballast, caulking the ship, taking in cargo and stowing sugar. The crew—one sailor having been discharged, and two new seamen signed on—was employed refitting the ship. Several other vessels, meanwhile, had put to sea: the *Equator*; the clippers *Westward Ho* (for Batavia) and the *Flying Fish*, which the *Revere* supplied with two barrels of flour, for Boston; the *Gem of the Ocean* for Boston and the *Golden City* for New York; the bark *Pilot* for Salem. The bark *Helen Baird* had received two pipes (800 lbs.) of bread from the *Revere*. On 26 May she started filling the water bins with 4,500 gallons of water; finished loading for Boston two days later; shipped two men as additional seamen; and took on 20 tierces of beef, 10 barrels of pork, 10 of flour, and 3,500 lbs. of bread for provisions.

More than 100 tons of ballast were added to the 1,569 tons of cargo already loaded, and valued there at $104,900—such items as hemp and hides, sapan wood, sugar and indigo to Howes and Crowell, and tortoise shells and glassware "to order," *i.e.*, to the master, in all probability (table 8). The charges at the port for stevedores discharging and loading, and for general use, totalled $325; paint for the "jack screws which had been in use for 50 days," $25. Finally, on 31 May the *Revere* proceeded down the Bay with a light, variable wind—now drawing 18 feet 10 inches aft, 18 feet 7 inches forward.[14]

Bound for the Lombok Straits, and heading generally south by southwest, she threaded her way through the maze of Philippine Islands—each one identified by Captain Hamilton in his log—working down the Mindanao shore and past the Nossa Sera Islands in the Celebes Sea. On 1 July the *Revere* hauled up to SSW, next day sighted the high peak on Lombok, and on 4 July cleared the south end of Bali. Having safely negotiated the islands and the straits, the crew could now unbend the chains and stow the anchors. Progress had been slow during that month among the volcanic outcroppings, but now they were free, in open water, where they could cover nearly two hundred sea miles a day, sailing west by south, with strong breezes and fine weather, and a ship occasionally in sight or even in company.

Table 8. Voyage 9 cargo: Manila to Boston

Product	Amount	Consignee	Value
glassware	3 cases	order	
hemp	342 bales	Howes & Crowell	9,906.00
	3,000 "	S. Austin	
	750 "	order	
	859 "	order	
hides	1,249	Grant & Daniels	
buffalo hides	100 bales	S. Austin	946.00
	50 bales	order	
indigo	26 cases	J. Pulna, Salem	200.00
	2 cases	Crocker & Sturgis	
	12 cases	Howes & Crowell	
	40 cases	order	
sapan wood	400 piculs	Howes & Crowell	400.00
sugar	160 bales	Howes & Crowell	2,550.00
tortoise shell	1 case	order	79.00
mdse	1 box/bale	order	
			$14,081.00

Total # of tons	1,569 cargo
plus ballast	127 tons
	1,696 tons

Sources: Boston Shipping List and Prices Current, 12 Oct 1853.
Note: The list is Capt. Hamilton's; the "value" figures appear in the consular quarterly "return of arrivals and departures of American vessels."

On 31 July a torrential storm broke—sharp lightning and thunder to the west; heavy rain; took in "all St^d sails, royals, flying jib, stay sails, fore & mizen topgallant sails; double reefed fore & mizen topsails and main topsail; furled mainsail, cross jack, spanker, & outer jib," and bore to the westward. Twelve hours later, all was calm, and on 2 August they sighted the land about Port Natal (Durban) and tacked to the south. More ships were in company; a number of fires visible on the land; and then, heavy gales, rain squalls, large seas, as the ship sailed in latitude 36.5 S almost due west for several days around the Cape of Good Hope, then a course mostly NNW and averaging only about sixty nautical miles a day for eight days. The captain kept a watchful eye on the leak about the bowsprit; he had put a casing around it and used every means to stop the leak, but without success.

Once past the Cape, light to moderate breezes and fine weather prevailed as they headed NW by N; then, strong breezes, all drawing sail set, for a record day's run of 226-1/2 miles. At last, on 26 August—87 days from Manila and 53 from Lombok—the crew got the larboard anchor over the bow and prepared to drop anchor off the island of St. Helena which was sighted at 4 P.M., bearing NW-½-N by compass, 20 miles distant. At 7:30 they anchored off James Town; early the next morning the captain sent on shore "2 pipes of bread, 5 tierces of beef, 1 barrel of pork, and 5 water casks." The consular report lists "general" cargo inward worth $140,000, and "assorted" cargo outward worth $100,000, without further identification,[15] in addition to the necessities of 1,100 gallons of water and fresh provisions.

At 5 P.M. the following day the ship was under way, making about 150 miles per day in fresh and moderate trades, frequently with all drawing sail set. The crew was occupied painting the outside of the ship, in 83-½° Fahrenheit temperature, and scraping and oiling the decks. Occasionally another ship was sighted, but none close enough to exchange signals. As they proceeded northward, the water turned perceptibly colder—from 72° at 6 P.M. one day, to 54° at noon on the following day (latitude 40.13 N, longitude 68 W). On the last full day on sea-time,[16] with strong gales and a large sea, they wore to the westward, then to the north (latitude 40.37 N, longitude 67.52 W), all sail set by the wind.

On 9 October 1853 at 8 A.M., they made Nauset Light, soon took on a pilot, and came into port at 3 P.M. "with larboard anchor & 30 fathoms chain, furled sails &c.; mid-night cloudy; so ends sea day of 36 hours to commence civil time, 131 days from Manila"—two days less than the first leg of the voyage, from Boston to San Francisco, and thirteen months from her starting point. Thus ends Captain Hamilton's log of the *Revere*'s first voyage around the world.

Journal of the *Revere* for the final leg of the around-the-world voyage into Boston. From the Manuscript Collection of Mystic Seaport Museum, Inc., Mystic, Connecticut. Used with permission.

3

IN PURSUIT OF CARGOES

1853-1865

The *Revere* spent much of the next four weeks undergoing repairs—
at Dillon's Dry Dock at Charlestown, at Matthews' Wharf, and, finally,
at Comey's Wharf. Then, on 11 November 1853 a new permanent register was issued because the ownership of shares had changed in part, and
a new master, Eben Sears, was given command. On the same day the
ship cleared on voyage number ten in her career, bound for Callao, Peru,
with a cargo of lumber and ice. She was probably chartered to Sampson
& Tappan for a load of guano on the return passage. Vernon Brown had
for some time been advertising his services as the only authorized agent
in Boston of Messrs. F. Barreda and Bro., procuring the highest rates of
freight from the Chincha Islands. The ship sailed on the twelfth but
remained at anchor in the harbor in rain and thick fog until 14 November.[1] Thence, according to the young second mate John Whidden, she
made "a quick run" to the equator and on to the latitude of the Falkland
Islands. The course was shaped to pass through the Strait of Le Maire,

View of Boston Harbor as seen from Fort Hill in the era of the *Revere*. Courtesy, Bostonian Society.

"between the island of Staten Land and Patagonia" at night, since the captain was "confident of his position," but on Friday, the 13th of January 1854, she fetched up on a reef off the southeasternmost tip of Tierra del Fuego.

> I was suddenly awakened, hearing four bells strike, and . . . the ship struck with a shock that brought my head in contact with a beam, causing me to see more stars than I ever imagined were made, . . . The ship was lying heeled well over on her port side, and with her yards thrown aback worked and pounded with such force that we expected every moment the spars would come about our ears. . . .
>
> Our only salvation lay in getting the ship afloat; unless we did, the probability was we should have to take to our boats and effect a landing on Staten Island, . . . taking the chance of being rescued by some passing vessel, or else make for the Chilean settlement of Sandy Point, Straits of Magellan.

Fortunately . . . as the strong gusts of wind swept down from the high land . . . the ship began to career and work, jumping until we trembled for the spars. . . . In the course of from twenty minutes to half an hour, she gave one final jump, and slid stern first into deep water. . . . Our steering apparatus was disabled, for a time the rudder was useless, both arms that worked the rudder-head with a system of cogs having been smashed. . . .

A consultation of all hands was called and the consensus of opinion was that it would be folly to attempt a passage around Cape Horn in our condition, the unanimous verdict being to . . . make Port Stanley, if possible, . . .

During the three days before we sighted Cape Pembroke [Falkland Islands], . . . all hands had cabin fare, canned meats and cabin stores were served out freely to the crew, as it was not known at what moment we might have to abandon ship. . . .

We sighted Cape Pembroke the third day, . . . The sounding-rod showed some nine feet of water in the hold just before rounding the cape. . . . The reach was narrow, and the shore was lined with penguins, standing on one leg, as regular as a troop of soldiers drawn up in line, which they very much resembled.

The American commercial agent, Captain Smyly, visited the ship immediately after she had dropped anchor at Stanley Harbor and arranged for the ship's stores to be removed to an old hulk that lay nearby, which would also serve as living quarters for the officers and crew. The lumber was sold at a good price to Dean and Co., the only local merchants, and the cakes of ice were hoisted out and dumped into the harbor "until the waters around the ship looked like a small section of the Arctic Ocean!"[2] When the damage was fully assessed, it turned out that the keel was nearly gone.

The garboard-streak was cut half through, lower part of rudder gone, the stem knocked off, and pieces gouged out of her bilge a fathom or two in length, not leaving but an eighth of an inch thickness of plank. The copper was wholly torn off her port side, with great copper bolts driven up through the keelson six inches and more. She was a sorry sight, and had she been loaded with any other cargo than ice and lumber, it would have been impossible to save her.

Her inward merchandise, never itemized in the Boston papers at sailing time, was listed in the consular return at Port Stanley as worth $40,000, and the cargo left behind worth $5,000.

The captain's formal protest gives the details as he reported them to the consul on 9 March:[3]

> By this public instrument of protest be it made manifest . . . that personally appeared before me, W. H. Smyly, commercial agent for the United States, Eben Sears, Master, [blank] Bind, Mate, [blanks] seamen who, being duly sworn, depose & say as follows:

> That on Monday Nov. the 14th they . . . proceeded to sea with double reefed topsails, wind NW, the ship being stout, staunch & strong and in every way fit to perform the voyage, and that nothing of importance having occurred until Friday 13 of January. Moderate breeze and cloudy weather; set the staysails at 10 p.m., took in the topmast staysail & royals at 2 a.m. The Ship struck on a reef about 20 miles from Cape St. Diego [latitude 54.38 S, longitude 65.05 W]; hove all aback and used every exertion to get the ship off. We remained there about half an hour. When she came off, sounded the pumps & found two feet of water, worked both pumps until noon, sounded & found & found [sic] four feet. Ends with moderate weather. . . .

> Jan. 14th, both pumps constantly going; found the ship gaining on us; sounded & found six feet water; found it necessary to make the nearest port, which was Port William, Falkland Islands. Wind SW, no obs., fine weather throughout. Jan. 15th, . . . both pumps continually going but yet the ship continues to gain on us. At 7 we found seven feet of water, and at noon there was eight feet, with both feet pumps constantly going. Got no obs. Monday the 16th, strong breezes & fine weather off the entrance of Port William; took in the light sails & double reefed the topsails; at 4 made sail; at 8, calm & foggy; at 10 a.m. see the beacon on Cape Penbrook. Ends calm.

Tuesday the 17th, got a pilot, wind S. at 4 p.m.; came to anchor in Port William, furled sails & found nine feet water in her; got a gang from the shore to pump, our own being nearly exhausted by constant pumping. Ends with fresh gales from the south. January 18th, the pumps constantly going by a gang of men from the shore. Succeeded in reducing her to two feet water. Friday 20, wind south, got under way and worked up to Port Stanley & came to and duly note his protest according to law, and the said master does hereby protest against the winds, weather, & each & every accident that has arose or that may arise out of the stranding of the said ship *Revere*.

[Appeared, *illegible*] & protested before me this 9 day of March in the year of our Lord one thousand eight hundred & fifty four.

In witness whereof I said commercial agent have set my hand & seal of office, this ninth day of March 1854.

On 22 March, some ten weeks after the disaster, the *Revere* sailed in ballast from the Falklands, "tight and sound as temporary repairs could make her," according to Whidden, with Captain Smyly's wife and child as passengers. They arrived in Boston fifty-eight days later, on 10 May, when the crew was paid off, and the ship went into dry dock for full repairs.[4] Sampson & Tappan apparently did not press charges, and there is no evidence that Howes & Crowell filed a case for general average distribution and apportionment to cover their own expenses. The one certainty is that Eben Sears was not in command of the next voyage.

After being detained at East Boston and at Charlestown, the *Revere* was again ready for sea and cleared on 1 July [voyage 11].[5] Two days later she sailed from Lewis Wharf under her new captain, Perry Bird, with twenty crewmen: Sampson & Tappan the agents, and Bolivia and Peru the announced destinations. Improbable as it seems, the *Revere* carried none of the mixed cargoes shipped from Boston during the week— shoes, chairs, oars, lumber, etc. She arrived at Callao in ballast on 11 November, with no stops en route. Her errand was to load a shipment of 1,800 tons of guano, consigned to Gibbs, Bright & Co. at Liverpool.[6] With the selling price of guano standing at about $50 per ton, and the freight charges at about $20 per ton, the revenues that would accrue to

Howes & Crowell as owners would compensate them generously even for passages in ballast between Boston and Callao and between Liverpool and Boston.[7]

Guano, used as a commercial fertilizer, had been exported from Peru to England since 1840, with Gibbs and Company as consignee, providing profits "intrinsically more valuable than the gold mines of California." Because the deposits of this partially decomposed excrement of seafowl were in the uninhabited portions of the offshore islands, and to a depth of sixty or seventy feet, they were wholly owned by the government, which consigned all the exports to a single house to which it paid a commission from the proceeds of sales—in effect, a government monopoly. The consignees had first to cover the initial expenses, usually by means of a "loan upon security of the shipments . . .

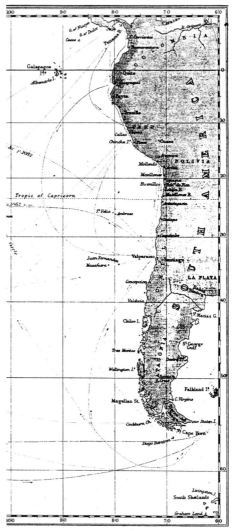

West coast of South America including Callao and the Chincha Islands

The amount of the loan, the rate of interest [5% in the final, 1857 contract before the Civil War], the duration of the contract, the markets to which it might be shipped, and the rate of commission [3%] varied with each contract. . . . The consignees agreed in addition to pay five per cent. interest on all balances due to the government remaining in their possession."

In 1851 Gibbs and Company, who had first inaugurated the trade in Baltimore, was replaced there by Felipe Barreda and Brother. The greatest demand for the fertilizer was from the cotton-growing states in the South, with Baltimore as the preeminent point for import and distribution. The annual imports there in the decade before the Civil War ranged from a low of 8,473 tons in 1858, when trade was temporarily diverted to New York, to a high of 54,134 tons in 1860—with a total value for the decade of over fourteen million dollars. But with the embargo on the southern ports and the cessation of Peruvian imports, in addition to the introduction of less expensive "phosphatic guanos" from other South American countries, the Baltimore agency closed its doors, at least for the duration. And after the war, the Peruvian government concentrated on the nitrate industry as a means of national revenue to substitute for guano.[8]

At the Chincha Islands, twelve miles off shore, the main source for the supply, some thirty ships were busy loading guano, and another eighteen or more were reported in the passages between Callao and the islands. The *Revere* departed on 3 February 1855, reportedly for Hampton Roads, but arrived at Liverpool on 25 May without any intermediate stops. When she sailed for Boston on 18 July, her cargo consisted of salt (3,277 sacks to E. Train & Co., 7,075 sacks "to order"), 25 tierces bleaching soda consigned to W. B. Reynolds, and 40 hogsheads, 3 tierces, 117 casks of merchandise to order. She arrived at Constitution Wharf, Boston harbor, on 27 August.[9]

Captain Bird soon found himself under indictment before the Massachusetts District Court in its September term for having allegedly beaten and wounded Alonzo Greene, a member of the crew. For want of a security deposit, the master was imprisoned, along with two crewmen, for twenty-one days—and reimbursed at the rate of one dollar each per day. When the case came to trial on 18 September, attorney I. Hardy Prince pleaded that his client was not guilty. Bird himself protested that his ship was ready to sail for Callao; that he was under contract and could not possibly wait for trial—he would lose his job and "suffer great pecuniary loss," and in any event he had no other job prospect. A jury of twelve—John Atwood, Jr., foreman—returned a verdict of not guilty.[10]

The captain was free to stay with his ship, which was now at Lewis Wharf. Rhoades & Matthews, sailmakers in Charlestown, had already made new main and mizzen topsails for the coming voyage, requiring 18 bolts of canvas @ $5 each.[11] After being cleared for voyage 12 on 18 September by Rollin Thorne & Co., the *Revere* waited at anchor in President Roads until a gale subsided.[12] Her destination was again Callao. Two days later she was sighted below Boston, having lost an anchor, some sails, and one of her topmasts, but the damage apparently was not severe enough to necessitate a return to port.

The sole news of the voyage was that the *Revere* had been spoken on 12 November southeast of Cape St. Roque (at latitude 6.58 S, longitude 34.10 W)—apparently a slower passage than Captain Hamilton's in 1852. She arrived at Callao on 19 January 1856, after a 120-day passage, with a cargo listed only as "ice, &c. &c."—684 tons of it![13] Since the end of the War of 1812 Frederic Tudor of Boston had been shipping ice to Jamaica under the monopoly granted him in the terms of the Treaty of Ghent (1814). Though the war had wiped out his pre-war trading, he persisted in his project—in debt and sometimes in jail. Having added Kingston and Havana, then the southern ports of the United States, and then Rio de Janeiro, in 1833 he made a trial adventure to Calcutta with 180 tons of ice, two-thirds of which arrived in good order— insulated with pine sawdust. "By 1841, although pushed by fifteen competitors and forced to lower the retail price to one cent a pound, [he] was able to pay off a debt of a quarter-million contracted by his early experiments."

Gradually Tudor expanded his market to include the large ports in South America and the Far East—"just in time to preserve Boston's East-India commerce from ruin." He was the consummate salesman, creating "an appetite for something you didn't even know you wanted." In the ten-year period 1847-1856, annual exports of ice from Boston more than doubled, to a total of 146,000 tons: 363 shipments, sent to 53 dif-

"Guano" or guanayes birds in their natural habitat in the Rock Pools of Lobos de Tierra, Peru (Robert Cushman Murphy, *Bird Islands of Peru*). Courtesy, Museum of Natural History, New York.

ferent places in the United States and abroad. Meanwhile "rum [exports] rose from four hundred thousand to over one million gallons, and three times as many boots and shoes left the port as ten years previously."[14] These three items constituted only a small portion of the week's total exports to Chile, which included even a steam engine—presumably all shipped on the *Revere,* the only vessel cleared for Callao, where her cargo was valued at $60,000, for delivery to Bolinton & Co. (table 9).

Having discharged her Boston cargo, she proceeded southward to Iquique, Chile, to pick up eight hundred tons of guano, valued there at $10,000. On returning to Callao she lost two crewmen by desertion "without Bird's knowledge or consent"; replacements were shipped, and on 26 February she sailed for Philadelphia.[15] She entered at Hampton Roads and was immediately cleared on 24 June, having "no guns" and twenty-one men, and reached her destination on 30 June. The cargo was officially checked in as 1,075 tons of guano, part of it contained in 1,200 bags, shipped by Barreda in Peru to F. Barreda & Bro. in Baltimore; 734

Table 9. Voyage 12 cargo: Boston to Callao

Product	Amount
almonds	1 case
barley	2 cases
beef	98 bbls
boots & shoes	88 cs
brooms	1,500
brushes	21 pkgs
candles	25 bxs
chairs	51 cases
child's carriages	3 cases
clocks	13 pkgs
coffee	51 bags
copperware	17 cases
cordage	10 coils
crackers	18 cases
cradles	24
domestics	49 pkgs
dresses	1 case
dry goods	10 cases
duck cloth	15 bolts
furniture	26 cases
glassware	2 tcs, 46 casks, 8 bxs
hams	5 tcs
hardware	261 pkgs
hats	2 boxes
I R goods	6 cases, etc.
ice	684 tons
ink	25 bxs
iron hoops	40 bdls
ladders	4
leather	8 rolls
lumber	51,000 ft.
macaroni	20 bxs
machinery	2 cases
masts, &c.	2 cases
nails	23 casks
oakum	14 bales
oars	84
oil carpeting	20 cases
pitch	50 bbls

(Continued on next page)

Table 9 (continued)

Product	Amount
rum	1,553 gals.
sheet lead	3 bxs
scales	26 cases
shovels & spades	396
soap	1,050 bxs
soy	16 bskts
spirits of turpentine	100 gals.
split peas	12 bbls
spun yarn	10 coils
steam engine	1
stoves	15 bxs
sugar	12 bbls
tacks	30 bxs
tar	25 bbls
tea	30 caddies
tobacco	10 boxes
trunks	40 nests
tubs	87 nests
vermicelli	10 bxs
vinegar	10 bbls
water kegs	1 crate
wheelbarrows	4 bxs
white lead	180 kegs
wood dippers	1 bbl.

Source: Boston Shipping List and Prices Current, 22 Sep 1855.

tons were in turn consigned to Sam. & I. Christian in Philadelphia. The cargo manifest also noted ship's stores in the amount of 10 barrels of salt, 2 barrels of flour, 700 pounds of bread, 50 of sugar, 10 each of coffee and tea. As of 1 July nothing remained on board subject to duty, though in fact—since the only cargo was the guano—there had been no dutiable item on arrival.[16]

On 19 August 1856 Captain Bird sailed on voyage 13 from Philadelphia for London, with a crew of nineteen. The most valuable single item in the mixed cargo was 2,493 barrels of flour, shipped for the

Table 10(a). Voyage 13 cargo: Philadelphia to London

Product	Amount	Shipper	Value
bark	21 hhds.	"clearance fee paid"	643.24
beef	125 tcs	W. M. Thackham	3,650.00
flour	100 bbls.	I. A. McCann Jr.	685.00
flour	2,493 bbls.	W. M. Thackham	16,204.00
flour	1,300 bbls.	William Paul	9,392.50
flour	121 bbls.	"clearance fee paid"	692.00
Indian corn	2 bbls, 2 casks, 17 bu.	John H. Graham	26.00
oilcake	150 bags (1127.325T)	W. M. Thackham	528.00
oilcake	1,103 bags (238,282 lbs)	W. M. Thackham	4,000.00
oilcakes	2,700 bags (537,632 lbs)	W. M. Thackham	9,250.00
quercitron bark	30 hhds.	"clearance fee paid"	816.41
rosin	386 bbls.	I. A. McCann Jr.	850.00
wheat	500 bags (1221 40/60 bu)	"clearance fee paid"	2,023.60
wheat	1,231 bags (3019 18/60 bu)	"clearance fee paid"	5,002.74
			$53,763.49

Sources: Outward foreign cargo manifest (National Archives, RG 36 Philadelphia); Boston Shipping List and Prices Current, 30 Aug 1856.

account of five suppliers of Paterson & McGrath and valued at $14,430, but priced for customs information at $68,194 (table 10a).[17] Having entered at London on 15 September, the *Revere* discharged her cargo and sailed on 30 September for Kronstadt, the port of St. Petersburg, Russia. She passed Elsinore, Denmark, on 6 October and reached the Russian port a week later, where she loaded a cargo that consisted entirely of locally produced goods (table 10b). A month later she sailed for Boston but ran ashore in the Öresund [Swedish] near Elsinore on 12 November. According to a telegraphic dispatch, a steamer had gone to her assistance, and she was examined by divers, who found some injury to her bottom,

Table 10(b). Voyage 13 cargo: St. Petersburg to Boston

Product	Amount	Consignee
bristles	4 cases	R. H. Wier
clean hemp	690 bales	Cunningham Bros.
crash	12 bales (23,112 lbs)	R. H. Wier
hemp yarn	5,642 lbs.	R. H. Wier
merchandise	2 bales	John Dwyer, merchant

Source: Boston Shipping List and Prices Current, 18 Apr 1857.

but the ship was still tight. Her cargo was discharged in order that repairs could be undertaken,[18] so it was not until 3 March 1857—after having undergone expensive repairs—that she finally put to sea again, with the entire cargo stowed back on board. It was valued in the consular return at $453.21, "the vessel having been under "[general] average" as a result of the disaster.[19] On 11 April 1857 the *Revere* finally returned to Boston, more than a year and a half after her departure for Callao.

She was idle at Commercial Wharf and shifted to Grand Junction Wharf before being cleared by Howes & Crowell for St. John, N.B., to load for a port in the Bristol Channel [voyage 14]. Her new captain was Matthew M. Rocko.[20] He sailed from Boston in ballast on 2 May 1857, arriving at St. John on 8 May. The cargo loaded there consisted of 55,400 feet of deals, 21,300 feet of deal ends, and 5,000 palings, valued at $4,320. On 22 May the ship sailed for Penarth Roads, Cardiff, landing her cargo in fact at Bristol on 2 June. From there she proceeded in ballast to Newport, Wales, to load for Rio: 1,084 tons of coal, valued at $2,164.

The crew was giving more than the usual amount of trouble. Eleven men deserted, and Captain Rocko was forced to lodge a complaint against two others—the chief and second mates. The acting consul at Bristol reported the case as one of frequent occurrence: Both his chief and second officers were "suffering from disease brought on by their own misconduct and . . . not actually laid up and unfit for duty [but] of little or no use in conducting the business of the ship." A consul could not

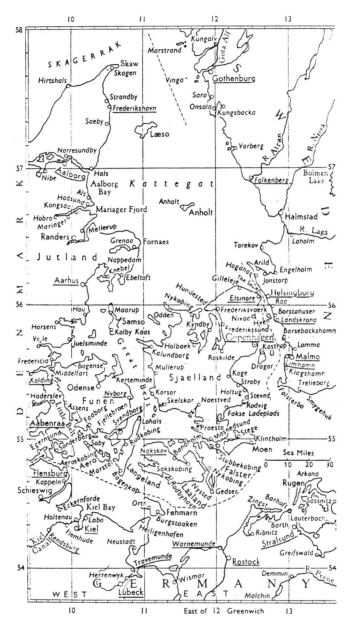

Chart of the Kattegat showing Elsinore and the area where the *Revere* grounded

usually discharge a seaman without demanding three months' extra pay for him, but Consul Ogden requested the power to discharge without pay.[21]

The *Revere* finally cleared Bristol with a full crew complement on 1 August 1857, arriving at Rio de Janeiro on 21 October. Almost immediately eight crewmen were jailed for refusing to do duty, and were released ten days later. On 3 December the ship sailed in ballast for Callao, arriving on 25 January 1858. For the job of loading Capt. Rocko shipped six "Cholos," Hispano-American seamen hired to load at the guano islands and return to Callao, which would take about six weeks. "They ship freely and are obedient, one or two generally speak English and pass the orders to the others, thus acting as boatswains. . . . They labor well, and bear the work of loading guano better than regular bred seamen do . . . on account of the strong smell of ammonia, and the dust." Another eight of the crew jumped ship at Callao, forcing the captain to sign on seven more men for the voyage to Torrevieja and Valencia before departure on 18 March 1858. The cargo of 1,193 tons of guano, insured for $20,000 and valued on the consular return at $36,000, fetched $25,770 on arrival at Valencia on 9 July 1858.[22]

Having discharged the fertilizer, the *Revere* proceeded on 27 August in ballast to Torrevieja, where she picked up 450 modines of salt for the Howes & Crowell account. The profit on that item alone was $1,783.27. The vessel was reported to have passed Gibraltar on 19 September, and on 20 October she arrived at Boston. The financial statement submitted to the owners after all accounts had been settled shows a net profit of $6,082.24 on the voyage (*see* appendix B.1).

Within a week of her arrival, Boston merchant Harry A. Peirce advertised "for freight or passage . . . the A1 Medford built ship *Revere*, 752 tons register, having one-half of her capacity engaged," to be dispatched in November for Valparaiso and Caldera.[23] During six weeks of repairs in various Boston yards, the largest bills incurred were $206 to the blacksmith, $300 to the sparmaker, and $1,061.25 for ship chandlery. There was also a cosmetic item: $51.50 for carving a figure head.

Captain Rocko had sailed with only eighteen men on his first voyage and carried the same number of crew when he sailed from Boston on 10 December 1858 on voyage 15.[24] The smaller crew is testimony to Captain Howes' claim that a ship of her size could dispense with at least two seamen, once she was equipped with the Howes' rig.

The nature of the cargo that merchant Peirce assembled is uncertain. The "assorted" cargo on board from Boston to Caldera was insured for $80,000—some of it cordage for Valparaiso.[25] After arrival there on 30 March 1859, seven sailors had deserted. Their replacements were signed on "to a port or ports in the Pacific Ocean and thence to a port of discharge in the United States, voyage not to exceed twelve calendar months." From Valparaiso the *Revere* proceeded to Caldera to discharge the balance of her Boston cargo, and thence to Cobra, Chile, to load copper ore. The shipment was negotiated by Samuel D. Crane & Co., of Boston, a branch of Loring & Co. of Valparaiso, to whom the commission was paid. The 23,000 quintals of ore, valued at $10,414.41, were consigned to David Keener at Baltimore, where the copper trade prospered. In the year 1858 alone, imports of the unwrought metal, worth over a million dollars, had accounted for 80 percent of that city's imports from Chile.[26] On the four-month voyage from South America to Baltimore (14 June to 8 October 1859) the *Revere* seems to have made no interim entrances. For the individual share-owners, the profits amounted to $417.45 per share on the basis of thirty-two shares; for Howes & Crowell as part-owners of the vessel, $5,426.85 for the ten-month period (*see* appendix B.2).

Surely the returns were better than those for the *Lizzie Oakford*, a slightly larger vessel in the Howes & Crowell fleet, which arrived at Antwerp in mid-July with a cargo of 1,700 tons of guano from Callao, having sprung a leak en route. The near-disaster required the attention of Osborn Howes, who happened to be in London with his wife. He later wrote in his biography that the matter was settled satisfactorily. The *Lizzie Oakford* sailed for Havana on 1 October with a cargo of Belgian bricks and hay—neither quantity nor value stated in the consul's return.[27]

Although nearly a year had elapsed since Captain Rocko had put in to Boston, his new orders sent the *Revere* south again, from Baltimore to Mobile in ballast on 5 November 1859 [voyage 16]. She arrived on 30 November and was cleared on 28 December for Le Havre, France. Her cargo, consisting solely of cotton [2,177 bales, totalling 1,137,294 lbs., and valued at $125,994.65] was shipped by P. Harding & Co. as agent for three Mobile shippers. The raw material had come into great demand for the cotton mills in Normandy, Flanders and Alsace, as well as in England. Thus, "when freights were good—and anything above a cent a pound made a 'saving voyage'"—it was economical for a merchant vessel to make one leg of the voyage in ballast. The *Revere* was fortunate. Having arrived at Le Havre on 4 February 1860 and discharged her cargo there, she proceeded to Cardiff on the 18th,[28] where she picked up 1,100 tons of coal consigned to Her Imperial Majesty's Government in Shanghai. On 4 April she set sail for China, where the Second China War was drawing to a close. Once there, the *Revere* would fight her own war with nature:[29]

> In the prosecution of her said voyage [the *Revere*] met with no unusual weather or remarkable accident, sail being set and taken in as occasion required and the pumps being regularly and properly attended to, until after the arrival at the port of Shanghai, China, namely Saturday August 18th, 1860. First part fresh breezes from S.E. and cloudy; sultry hot during the night; hard squalls, thunder and lightning; heavy rain. At 3 A.M. on the flood, heavy squalls; the ship dragged both her anchors, went onshore on soft level mud, laid there till the next flood without straining or injuring the hull. At day light, set the jack for a pilot, a gentleman named Captain Bally called on board saying the ship was perfectly safe on the slack of the ebb; took the stream anchor with 90 fathoms of hawser out to get the ship off on the flood. At 11 A.M. the flood tide set in very rapid—at . . . least 8 miles per hour. The tide took her on the port bow, swung off shore, dragged her anchor having 35 fathoms on the best bower [anchor], 90 fathoms on the other; went into collision with the ship "*G. B. Carr* [633T, Swedish]" and could not avoid it; sustained a great deal of damages. Carried away our mainmast, main yard jibboom, sprung main topsail yard and starboard fore and topmast backstays, topgallant and Royal Cat and chafed fore and main

lifts and braces and boom irons and main truss and sling bands and
other small iron more or less carried away the wreck; hove the port
anchor up and stream anchor and moored her again with 45 on the flood
and 35 on the ebb. No pilot came off.

This formal "marine note of extended protest" was filed by Captain Rocko with Consul S. G. Smith on 29 August, in which he and
witnesses from the ship "declare and say: That [they] used their utmost
endeavors to preserve the said ship and cargo from all manner of loss,
damage, or injury. Wherefore . . . all losses [etc.] ought to be borne by
those to whom the same by right may appertain by way of average or
otherwise . . . "[30]

When the repairs were finally accomplished, a cargo of peas,
cotton, etc., produced or manufactured in Ningpo and consigned to Frazar
& Co., was on-loaded. The *Revere* sailed on 1 November, but not before
one man was discharged and fourteen shipped, presumably because an
equal number had deserted at Shanghai. Her destination was listed as
Hongkong, but on 22 November she arrived at Canton, where the Ningpo
cargo was discharged, and on 11 December she proceeded in ballast to
Manila, arriving on 20 December 1860. When she sailed west for Boston
on 9 January 1861 her cargo consisted entirely of Philippine products,
valued at $83,425 (table 11).[31]

On 23 January she was reported as having passed Anjer, Java,
a favorite navigational landmark and supply center, destroyed in 1883 by
the eruption of Krakatoa; it is unlikely, however, that she stopped since
she had been so recently provisioned. Three months later, on 25 April
1861, the *Revere* docked at Lombard's Wharf in Boston, after an absence
of two years and four months.

Thayer & Peabody were the agents for the Howes & Crowell
charter from St. John, N.B., when the *Revere* was cleared at Boston in
ballast on 9 May 1861 on voyage 17.[32] The voyage to St. John had taken
only five days, but it was not until 7 June that Captain Rocko set sail for
Valparaiso with a cargo of Maine sawn lumber valued at $15,552 and
insured for $12,000. Two months out, she was spoken off the coast of
Brazil, south of the Tropic of Capricorn, and on 16 September she arrived

Table 11. Voyage 16 cargo: Manila to Boston

Product	Amount	Consignee
cigars	20,000	order
hemp	1,220 bales	G. B. Upton
hemp	1,430 do.	G. A. Gardner
hemp	1,300 do. order	
hide cuttings	200 bales order	
hide cuttings	125 bales	G. Wiggin & Co.
sapan wood	425 piculs	Howes & Crowell
sugar	9,376 bags	Bates & Co.

Source: Boston Shipping List and Prices Current, 8 May 1861.

at Valparaiso where some of the lumber was discharged. The remainder of the cargo was off-loaded at Coquimbo, then the ship proceeded in ballast to Cobija, arriving on 23 October.[33]

When she set out for Liverpool two months later, on 24 December 1861, her outward cargo was 1,134 tons of guano from Pachoca, Peru, valued at $17,000 and insured for $15,000. The value on the consul's return at Callao on 7 January 1862, en route, doubled to $34,030—a figure that seems grossly exaggerated inasmuch as the amount realized at Liverpool was apparently only $16,068.66. At Callao ten men were shipped for the voyage, "via ports in South America," *i.e.*, eastward. Cargo discharged at Liverpool after arrival there on 23 April included 27,583 barrels of grain, 657 tierces of lard and 301 of bacon and 3,600 staves—in addition to the guano.[34] On 28 May her sole cargo outward was 970 tons of salt—3,905 hogsheads for Albert P. Clark, Boston salt merchant, and 50 hogsheads for Baker & Morrill, commission merchants in Boston and New York—for a net profit of $2,730.87 (table 12).

After arrival at Boston on 7 July 1862 negotiations were undertaken for the sale of the *Revere*. In the heyday of clipper-ship building (1850-1855) Howes & Crowell had acquired the ships *Hamlet* and *Rival*, the clipper ships *Climax* (which sank in 1855) and *Ringleader*, the medium clippers *Fleetwing* and *Osborn Howes*, the extreme clipper *Robin*

Hood for use in the booming East India Trade—all of them larger and faster than the *Revere*, all of them more costly to build, outfit and maintain. Their owners depended for profit on freight and passage money, not on speculative cargoes of their own. By the year 1857, however, California had developed markets of its own, and the East India merchants had glutted the Boston market with Calcutta goods, which resulted in a financial crisis and depression that lasted for two years. During this period the cotton market in England was flooded to the point where some cargoes were trans-shipped back to New England. Then, just as conditions reverted to normal, the Civil War erupted, which, in turn, hastened the substitution of steam for sail and brought about another change in the shipping industry. In addition, the clipper ships, which had been "our Gothic cathedrals, our Parthenon . . . flashed their splendor around the

Table 12. Voyage 17 cargo: Liverpool to Boston

Account Sales of Liverpool Salt by Howes & Crowell for a/c of owners of ship *Revere*.

Albert P. Clark	Cash	
3905 hhds @ 1.94	7,575.70	
Baker & Morrill (less duty)		
50 hhds @ 1.25	62.50	
labor on same	7.50	
Charges		7,645.70
Prem. ins. Liverpool to Boston		
$4,000 @ 1-3/4%	700.00	
Cost of sale £382.3 @ 4.80	1,834.32	
Duties	2,667.08	
Wharfage 4 x 3905	156.20	
Comm on sales (called)		
7,489.50 @ 2-12%	187.23	
		4,915.83
		2,730.87

E. & O.E., Boston, Aug 21st 1862
  Howes & Crowell
  for W. P. Ellison

Source: Yarmouth Port Historical Society; microfilm, courtesy International Marine Archives, Nantucket, Massachusetts.

world, then disappeared with the finality of the wild pigeon." They had
fulfilled their purpose of "speed to the gold fields at any price or risk.
When that was no longer an object, no more were built." And, with
Lincoln's embargo of the southern ports in 1861, including even Baltimore, once a good outlet for guano, all manner of shipping suffered from
lack of both outward cargo and markets for return loads.[35]

Now, in mid-1862, for the requirements of Osborn Howes and
Nathan Crowell, the *Revere*'s day was past. With the other owners (Eben
Howes, Isiah Crowell, David Kelley, David K. Akin, the widow of Daniel
Crocker, N. S. Simpkins, Silas Baker and the executors of George Lovell's
estate), but excepting Oliver Eldridge, they sold their combined interests
to three Boston merchants of the firm of Baker & Morrill, owners of a
large fleet of sailing vessels. Ezra H. Baker and Charles J. Morrill,
together with Benjamin Hough of Gloucester, paid $22,500 for thirty of
the thirty-two outstanding shares.[36] The value of the ship, then, may be
reckoned at $24,000.

By the time the war was over, a number of the vessels owned by
Howes & Crowell, and by other Boston merchants as well, had been sold
to foreigners, under pressure from the high cost of insuring against war
risks and the advantages that accrued to foreign competitors in procuring
charters. Though Boston's shipping suffered, Howes & Crowell were
able to continue operations: in 1864 their credit was reported as first rate
by R. G. Dun & Co., and their assessment on the Boston tax-rolls stood
at $90,000.[37] And, as a measure of the esteem in which Osborn Howes
himself was held in the maritime community, it may be noted that he was
elected president of the Boston Marine Society and served in that capacity
from November 1860 to November 1863.

The *Revere* underwent minor repairs and commenced loading at
Battery Wharf, then at East Boston and at Charlestown, before sailing
for Rio de Janeiro on 22 August 1862 [voyage 18]. During her stay she
was metalled* and presumably remeasured prior to issuance of her new

---

* This refers to the practice of nailing copper plating or sheathing to the underwater hull
of wooden vessels to prevent teredo worm infestation, which was common before the
development of paints which had the same effect. Of course, each ton of sheathing on the
hull meant a proportionate loss of carrying capacity.

Osborn Howes' certificate of membership in the Boston Marine Society

permanent register on 21 August.[38] Her new captain was Nathaniel P. Gibbs, who had been involved in an international incident in 1854 as captain of the brig *John R. Dow.*

Philo H. Shelton, an enterprising Boston merchant, had dispatched Gibbs to West Indian waters in search of guano, which Gibbs found in a substantial deposit on Venezuela's Aves Island, nearly one hundred miles north of Caracas. He landed and explored, then took formal possession and returned to Boston to report his discovery. On receipt of the news, Mr. Shelton and others sent several vessels, along with laborers, mechanical tools, lumber and materials, implements and vehicles for gathering and loading the guano. A settlement was built, with tenements for the families who had accompanied the men, provision stores, cisterns for water, fences, wharves, and even a Liberty Pole. From June until December 1854 the Bostonians occupied the islet, renamed "Shelton's Isle," and shipped cargoes of guano to Europe and the United States.

Early in December 1854 the Venezuelan government sent a warship and troops to put an end to the occupation. At bayonet point the Americans were driven off, leaving all their equipment behind. Gibbs had signed a document that was erroneously misinterpreted in translation as allowing him to take guano without charge or molestation. It was in fact "a regular formal military Capitulation of the island," which he of course had no authority to sign. Nor was the Venezuelan government within its rights in obtaining a paper "by military duress, combined with trick and fraud, from an agent not authorized to sign, or to give or to take it." The claims subsequently preferred to the State Department by Mr. Shelton and by Messrs. Sampson & Tappan, who also had an interest in the operation, amounted to $341,000 and had still not been adjudicated fourteen months later. Captain Gibbs was certainly "not competent to compromise the national rights of the United States enuring from the discovery of the guano, and possession of the island by its citizens," and the actions on both sides were condemned as "a rare compound of diplomatic effrontery and stupidity."[39]

Eight years later Venezuela was under no threat from Gibbs en route to Rio, which he reached on 14 October 1862 with a cargo of 700 tons of "ice, &c. &c." This probably included the 178,582 feet of lumber and "sundries" listed in the consular return, and perhaps also the twenty sewing machines and other consumer items among the week's exports from Boston to Brazil (table 13a). The *Revere* was cleared a month later in ballast for the East Indies, and arrived on 12 February 1863 at Singapore,[40] where she began loading general cargo for Penang and New York. Having sailed on 27 March, she arrived at the Malayan port of Penang by 10 April and one week later was cleared for New York with a cargo consigned to H. P. Sturgis & Co., Boston merchants with offices at 80 State Street and in New York at 73 South (table 13b).[41]

Hardly had the *Revere* arrived at her East River dock on 8 September 1863 than negotiations were under way for yet another change of ownership. Eldridge retained his 1/16 interest; Ezra Baker, Hough, and Morrill reduced their holdings to 1/16 each, receiving $22,500 for the 12/16th that they sold. Laban Howes, now master, who had taken the Howes

& Crowell *Fleetwing* to San Francisco on her maiden voyage in 1854, was now the largest shareowner; Henry V. Schenck of New York bought 8 of the 64 shares, as did Stevens, Baker & Co. (Judah Baker Jr., Levi Stevens, and C. C. Baker) of San Francisco. The remaining shares were held by Cape-Codders and younger New York residents, mostly from Cape Cod families and related to some of the previous owners: Josiah Nickerson, William E. Baker, Captain William F. Howes; and, from New York, David Lincoln, George Mariner, Nymphus Hall, Darius Crowell and the brothers Howes and Alpheus Baker. The news report that the ship was sold for $27,000 was short of the mark: although $22,500 changed hands, the purchase price of all the shares would have been $30,000.[42]

With the formalities over, Laban Howes set sail for San Francisco on 26 November 1863 as owner/master of the *Revere*, c/o Merchant & Carman [voyage 19]. Her chief cargo of 1,101 tons of coal was consigned to A. B. Forbes; to the master: 25 half-barrels of mackerel, 200 half-cases of oil, and 181 kits of cranberries. There were no passengers. On 29 April 1864, after a very calm passage, with fine pleasant weather

Table 13(a). Voyage 18 cargo: Boston to Rio de Janeiro

Product	Amount
brooms	360
brushes	144
carpet bags	12
catawba wine	3 doz.
chairs	247 cases
cigars	2,000
Daguerrean goods	2 bxs
enam. cloth	12 yds.
flannel	33 yds.
hardware	35 pkgs
ice	700 tons
India rubber	19 bskts
lumber	175,582 ft.
rubber bands	1-1/2 gross
sewing machines	10

Source: <u>Boston Shipping List and Prices Current</u>, 30 Aug 1862.

throughout, the *Revere* reached San Francisco, where she was duly registered on a temporary certificate.[43]

Laban Howes' nephew, Barzillai, took over as captain when the *Revere* sailed for "Angelos" (Port Angeles, Washington Territory) on 23 May 1864, under a new register dated 20 May [voyage 20].[44] Two of his crew were also natives of Cape Cod: Zenas Howes, first mate, and Nymphus Crocker, second mate. After more than two months loading at Tekalet (Port Gamble, Washington Territory), the ship sailed from Puget Sound for Manila, consigned to Stevens, Baker & Co., one-eighth owners of the ship. In Manila four seamen were added, their "wages to be paid in gold or currency according to payment of balance of the crew." They set sail on 24 December—having first been announced as loading for New York, and later for San Francisco, which they reached on 23 March 1865, with a large cargo (table 14). The voyage took eighty-six days—thirty of them in the China Sea, with heavy and rough weather to the meridian [international dateline], which resulted in split sails, stove in bulwarks, parted lower main rigging, started planking off the stern and parted seams in the hull—to such an extent that the vessel was leaking

Table 13(b). Voyage 18 cargo: Penang to New York

Product	Amount
cabobs	120 bags
cassia	58 cases
cloves	11 bags
coffee	1,093 bags, 500 pockets
gambier	5,029 bales
hides	462 cases
India rubber	19 bskts
nutmegs	138 cases
pearl sago	142 bxs
pepper	7,503 bags
rattan	10,561 bdls
sapan wood	3,023 piculs
tapioca	357 bxs
tin	3,282 slabs

Source: <u>New York Shipping and Commercial List</u>, 9 Sep 1863.

badly. In addition, soon after departure from Manila, one seaman died of appendicitis.

Following remeasurement in San Francisco, which noted the tonnage at 829-33/100 tons (762-28/100 "under tonnage deck" and 67-05/100 "enclosures on the upper deck") instead of the former 734-12/95 tons, a new, temporary register was issued on 17 April 1865.[45] The increase in tonnage, and the higher fees would raise the port duties for which the ship would be annually liable.

Two days later the *Revere* departed on her first Pacific voyage [number 21], bound for Nanaimo, British Columbia, to take on coal for San Francisco. She carried a crew of fourteen—the smallest number yet shipped. Standard shipping articles stipulated that no sheath knives or profane language were allowed on board, nor any grog—language that remains in the articles even today. Wages ranged from $55 per month for Nymphus Crocker, now first mate, to $35-$50 for the seamen. Captain Barzillai Howes received $100 per month for his services. With 1,100 tons of coal loaded for Dickson, De Wolf & Co. of San Francisco—the first of many such cargoes for this company—the ship made a quick passage of fifteen days from Nanaimo, arriving in San Francisco on 17 June.[46]

Table 14. Voyage 20 cargo: Manila to San Francisco

Product	Amount	Consignee
cigars	20 cases	C. A. Lowe & Co.
hay lashings	200 cases	San Francisco Cordage Co.
hemp	1,000 bales	"
sugar	24,480 bags	Wm. T. Coleman & Co.

Source: Daily Alta California, 23 Mar 1865.

4

COASTWISE IN
THE PACIFIC

1865-1881

W ithin a month the news was out that the *Revere* had been sold once again—this time for about $18,000—to "Mastic & Kenrich" at San Francisco, to be employed in the coastwise lumber trade. The bill of sale, dated 12 September 1865, identifies the sellers as Stevens, Baker & Co. and others, the purchase price $17,750 in full. The new owners were John Kentfield, Levi B. Mastick and Calvin Paige, each of whom purchased a one-third interest in the vessel.[1]

John Kentfield left Oyster Bay, Long Island, in 1849 and soon established himself in San Francisco as a manufacturing, lumber and shipping merchant. With his brother George he first acquired two sailing vessels for transporting hay and lumber to various ports on the California coast. Later, as Kentfield & Co. in San Francisco, they operated the Island Mill on an island in Humboldt Bay and the Jones Mill at Eureka, constructed the South Bay logging railroad in Humboldt County, and by the 1870s had become one of the largest shipping firms on the Pacific

Coast. Although owning only a one-third interest in the ship, they were usually identified as the owners of the *Revere*, the eighth major addition to their fleet since 1857.[2]

Levi B. Mastick arrived in California in 1853 and, with his brother, Seabury, was part owner of the firm of S. L. Mastick & Co., manufacturers and dealers in lumber at their Port Discovery Mills in Washington Territory. They were also proprietors of the Humboldt and Puget Sound packets, with offices on the pier at 10 Stewart Street in San Francisco, where Kentfield was also a tenant. In 1865 Levi Mastick was a member of the San Francisco Board of Education. He later retired, to engage in raising fruit in San Jose, but held his shares in the *Revere* until January 1878, when they were bought up by John Kentfield's son and heir, Edward.[3]

Of the three new owners of the ship, Calvin Paige, born in 1827 in Hardwick, Massachusetts, was the most recent arrival in the city. He appears in a San Francisco city directory first in 1865, as a real estate broker with an office at 205 Battery Street. He remained a partner until 1882, by which date he, too, had gone into farming. At that time he sold his shares in the *Revere* to her master, Captain James McIntyre. Paige later moved to New York, where he died in 1909.[4]

More than twelve years had passed since the *Revere*'s first arrival at San Francisco, in January 1853—one of the 1,028 vessels, 634 of them American, to have arrived in that year, which also saw the number of immigrants by sea increase by a net of three thousand persons, after departures, and the shipping tonnage to 407,000 tons. In the intervening years one gold rush subsided, another flared up and fizzled, and exploration for silver in Nevada presently claimed the largest share of mining activity in the area. Now, in 1865, the city's population stood at about 119,000—more than double that of 1853—with more people departing than immigrating. The city's port facilities had steadily enlarged, with the filling of low lands along the bay shore and the building of long piers into deep water. The tonnage arriving from domestic Pacific ports now totalled 283,000 tons, about half of it in "coasters," *i.e.*, vessels sailing between American ports on the Pacific—and this would be the role of the Kentfield & Co. ship *Revere*.

Beginning as early as 1850, when the Pope & Talbot firm selected Port Gamble on Puget Sound as the site for its first mill, lumber emerged as the first and leading industry in the Washington Territory. In the decade that followed, many of the great sawmills were established in that area: the Port Blakely Mill across the Sound from Seattle, and extensive mills in Port Discovery Bay, at Seabeck on Hood's Canal, at Utsalady, Tacoma, Bellingham Bay and elsewhere. The Bellingham Bay area had also yielded some coal, but it was chiefly the mines on Vancouver Island, British Columbia, that attracted the San Francisco dealers and fostered the growth of the coal mining industry in the Canadian province.[5]

Over the next fifteen years the *Revere*'s schedule varied only slightly: ship a crew, load provisions and 250 tons of ballast at San Francisco; discharge ballast and load supplies as necessary and cargo as ordered: coal at Nanaimo or Departure Bay, British Columbia, or lumber at Port Townsend or Port Discovery, both in Washington Territory; return to San Francisco; discharge cargo and crew, undertake repairs and maintenance jobs in port, be ready for the next shuttle assignment. The consignees, too, were "regulars": Mastick and Kentfield/Rosenfeld at the outset; then Dickson, De Wolf & Co.; Berryman & Doyle; Dunsmuir, Diggle & Co. And the round-voyage averaged about two-and-a-half months; the San Francisco-to-Puget Sound run, about twenty days.

Because the voyages from 1865 on adhered so nearly to a timetable and were generally uneventful, a tabulation by voyage will suffice to give routine information on dates, ports-of-call, consignees, names of occasional passengers, and remarks on the weather (table 15). Many of the later voyages, however, merit some comment, whether on account of their unusual routes, or because financial statements have survived that throw some light on the economic aspects of the cargo business, or even for the purpose of detailing the story of a disaster.

In the eighteen years of Kentfield ownership, there were only three regular captains: J. W. Brown, James McIntyre, and Thomas Conner, and it was J. W. Brown, a native of New York and in 1863 first mate of

Seamen's Bond.

Know all Men by these Presents, That we,

James Mc Intyre

Master or Commander of

the _____ *Ship* _____ called the _____ "*Revere*"

now lying in the **District of Puget Sound,** and *B. S. Pettygrove,*

of Port Townsend, W. T,

are held and firmly bound unto the United States of America, in the full and just sum of **Four Hundred Dollars,** money of the United States; to which payment, well and truly to be made, we bind ourselves jointly and severally, our joint and several heirs, executors and administrators, firmly by these presents.

Sealed with our Seals, and dated this **First** *day of* **July** *One Thousand Eight Hundred and Sixty* **Seventy two**

Whereas the above bounden Master, *James Mc Intyre*

hath delivered to the Collector of the Customs for the **District of Puget Sound,** Washington Territory, a verified list, containing, as far as he can ascertain them, the names, places of birth, residence, and description of the persons who compose the company of the said _____ *Ship* _____

called the _____ *Revere*

now lying in the said District, of which he is at present Master, or Commander; of which list the said Collector has delivered to the said **Master** a certified copy.

Now, the Condition of this Obligation is such, That if the said Master shall exhibit the aforesaid certified copy of the list to the first boarding officer, at the first Port in the United States at which he shall arrive on his return thereto, and then and there also produce the persons named therein to the said boarding officer, except any of the persons contained in the said list, who may be discharged in a foreign country, with the consent of the Consul, Vice-Consul, Commercial Agent, or Vice-Commercial Agent, there residing, signified in writing under his hand and official Seal, to be produced to the Collector of the said District within which he may arrive as aforesaid, with the other persons composing the crew, as aforesaid, or who may have died or absconded, or who may have been forcibly impressed into other service, of which satisfactory proof shall be then also exhibited to the said last mentioned Collector; then and in such case the obligation shall be void and of no effect, otherwise it shall abide and remain in full force and virtue.

Stamped, Sealed, and Delivered in presence of

P. D. Mood
W. M. Harned

James Mc Intyre
P. S. Pettygrove

The seaman's bond is a document by which the captain of the vessel guarantees that he is presenting an accurate crew list to the collector of customs for the port in question. Courtesy, National Archives, Seattle.

the *S.S. Panama,* who was master when the *Revere* sailed in ballast for the Puget Sound area [voyage 22]. The cargo of lumber shipped from Port Discovery, Washington Territory, was consigned to S. L. Mastick.[6] On the next voyage [number 23] she brought 1,250 tons of coal from Nanaimo, British Columbia, to San Francisco for the account of Rosenfeld & Co.[7] Immediately after her return, enrollment papers were issued, permanently changing the ship's district from New York to San Francisco and naming her new captain and owners.[8] It was not, however, until 9

Invoice from Rothschild & Co. of Washington Territory for goods purchased to the account of the *Revere.* Courtesy, Bancroft Library.

March 1871 that her official number, 21620, and the call letters HWRC appear on a San Francisco enrollment.

In April 1866 it was James McIntyre, a native of Scotland and former captain of the bark *Massachusetts,* who became master [voyage 26].[9] He continued in that capacity until April 1883 (the longest term of any of the *Revere*'s captains), except for a period of about sixteen months, when Kentfield employed him, in command of the *Discovery,* to reconnoiter in Wilmington and San Diego, where the railroad was being developed. Dickson, De Wolf & Co., a regular customer during the second year of operations, was importing about 1,250 tons of coal per voyage. Then, from May 1867 until November 1875, Mastick seems to have exercised a virtual monopoly—attendant perhaps on principal ownership of the Port Discovery Mill as well as partial ownership of the *Revere*—and regularly shipped about 500,000 feet of lumber and 200,000 or more laths, also piles or spars, and ships' knees, from Port Discovery. By the summer of 1870, however, the general economic depression in the country had affected the western lumber business, so that both ships and mills were operating less than full time. Cargoes were augmented with potatoes, and on one voyage [number 68] with eight rolls of India matting and

Receipt for cargo issued at Port Discovery after loading lumber and lath aboard the *Revere*. Courtesy, Bancroft Library.

one bale of bear, deer, and coon skins. That particular voyage ended in San Francisco in mid-March with the *Revere* being stuck in the mud for several days and, along with eight other square-rigged vessels, having to unload over a million feet of lumber into the lighters lying between Mission Street Wharf and Larue's Wharf.[10]

For the first time in eight years the routine was broken in July 1873. New shipping articles prior to the 14 July departure from San Francisco [voyage 71] specified that the *Revere* go to Port Discovery to load cargo for San Diego, where lumber and piles were in demand for

(Text continues on page 95)

Table 15. Coastwise voyages in the Pacific

Note: All dates of departure and arrival were from San Francisco.

Voyage	Departure Arrival	Ports of Call	Consignee/Cargo	Memoranda
22	30 Jun '65 21 Aug '65	Port Discovery	S. L. Mastick lumber	light NW, calm, fog
23[a]	1 Sep '65 25 Nov '65	Nanaimo	Kentfield/Rosenfeld 1,250T coal	light S & SE; calm; strong N
24[b]	29 Nov '65 7 Feb '66	Port Discovery	S. L. Mastick 600M ft. lumber	
25	16 Feb '66 10 Apr '66	Port Discovery	S. L. Mastick 600M lumber	
26	18 Apr '66 19 Jun '66	Nanaimo	Rosenfeld 1,276 T coal	light SE; light W; light SE & SW; strong NW
27[c]	29 Jun '66 19 Aug '66	Nanaimo	Dickson, de Wolf & Co. coal	light NW
28	29 Aug '66 20 Oct '66	Nanaimo	Dickson, de Wolf & Co. coal	light NW; fine weather
29[d]	3 Nov '66 2 Jan '67	Nanaimo	Dickson, de Wolf & Co. 1,170 T coal	strong southerly winds outward: flour 100M sacks, 200 qtr. sacks; val. $571.25
30[e]	15 Jan '67 25 Feb '67	Nanaimo	Dickson, de Wolf & Co. 1,290 T coal	strong S & SW; NW 21 Jan, man overboard

[a] John Rosenfeld was a prominent shipping and commission merchant of San Francisco and a grain shipper. He held the agency of the Vancouver Coal and Land Company at Nanaimo, British Columbia, from 1856 and was later vice-president of the Pacific Coast Steamship Company. He was active in public affairs as president of the board of City Fire Commissioners and a member of the board of the State Harbor Commissioners (Hittell, *Commerce*, 205, 767, 783).

[b] *Daily Alta California*, 8 Feb 1866, mistakenly notes arrival of the *Revere* "from Baltimore, coal to O. Eldridge," a former share holder.

[c] Dickson, De Wolf & Co. were dealers in bags and champagne, grain shippers, importers, lumber manufacturers, shipping merchants, and owners of Hastings sawmill on the mouth of the Burrard Inlet, near the mouth of the Fraser River in British Columbia (Hittell, *Commerce*, 590, 753, 760, 767, 769, 774, 783).

[d] National Archives, RG 36 San Francisco, returned crew list, 2 Jan 1867.

[e] Ibid., returned crew list, 25 Feb 1867.

Voyage	Departure Arrival	Ports of Call	Consignee/Cargo	Memoranda
31	8 Mar '67 24 Apr '67	Nanaimo	Dickson, de Wolf & Co. 1,250 T coal	SE gales
32	20 May '67 7 Jul '67	Port Townsend Port Discovery	S. L. Mastick 550 M ft. lumber 250 M laths	SE; light NW pass.: S. McGill & wife
33[a]	18 Jul '67 27 Aug '67	Port Townsend Port Discovery	S. L. Mastick 600 M ft. lumber	
34	4 Sep '67 22 Oct '67	Port Discovery	S. L. Mastick 560 ft.lumber	
35	29 Oct '67 5 Dec '67	Port Townsend Port Discovery	S. L. Mastick lumber	pass.: Mrs. G. B. Hansell Mrs. A. Hornsey
36	16 Dec '67 30 Jan '68	Port Townsend Port Discovery	S. L. Mastick 550 M ft. lumber 200 M laths	
37	8 Feb '68 18 Mar '68	Port Townsend Port Discovery	S. L. Mastick 500 M ft. lumber	strong SE & SW pass.: S. Baxter R. E. Ryan
38[b]	28 Mar '68 11 May '68	Port Townsend Port Discovery	S. L. Mastick 550 M ft. lumber 150 M laths	strong W'ly, light NW pass.: John Pugh
39	14 May '68 9 Jun '68	Port Townsend Port Discovery	S. L. Mastick 550 M ft. lumber 220 M laths	variable winds & calms
40	27 Jun '68 9 Aug '68	Port Townsend Port Discovery	S. L. Mastick 550 M ft. lumber 200 M laths	light NW pass.: Mrs. Hubbs & 2 children, J.C.H. Rothschild, Henry Humer
41[c]	15 Aug '68 5 Oct '68	Port Townsend Port Discovery	S. L. Mastick boards, flooring, fencing	12 Sep: 2 crew added

[a] Another survey was filed in August 1866 (Lloyd's *Register* for 1868).
[b] Benjamin S. Pettygrove, age 21, appears on the crew list. He was the son of Francis W. Pettygrove, a native of Calais, Maine, and a founder of Portland, Oregon, who had moved to Puget Sound in 1852 and was also a founder of Port Townsend (*Washington Historical Quarterly* 5 [1914]:4). In 1867 Capt. McIntyre married Sophie Pettygrove, a daughter of Francis (James G. McCurdy, *By Juan de Fuca's Strait* [Portland, Oregon, 1937].
[c] Kentfield Papers 90/1.

Voyage	Departure Arrival	Ports of Call	Consignee/Cargo	Memoranda
42	9 Oct '68 11 Dec '68	Port Townsend Port Discovery	S. L. Mastick lumber	
43[a]	22 Dec '68 4 Feb '69	Port Townsend Port Discovery	S. L. Mastick 550 M ft. lumber 220 M laths	at California Dry Dock pass.: M. Branard 21 Jan, 2 crew added
44	13 Feb '69 4 Apr '69	Victoria Port Townsend Port Discovery	S. L. Mastick 550 M ft. lumber 200 M laths	heavy SE gales; strong NW winds. 22-23 Mar: 3 seamen added. pass.: M. Branard
45	9 Apr '69 27 May '69	Port Townsend Port Discovery	S. L. Mastick 260 M ft. lumber 22,500 ft. piles 200 M laths	light SW; fresh NW pass.: Mrs. F. W. Petty- grove, Mrs.L.B. Hastings
46	4 Jun '69 21 Jul '69	Port Townsend Port Discovery	S. L. Mastick 560 M ft. lumber 20 M laths	
47	29 Jul '69 7 Sep '69	Port Townsend Port Discovery	S. L. Mastick 500 M ft. lumber 20 M laths	pass.: Mrs. N.D. Hill & 3 children, Mrs. H. Smith, 3 children. W.Graham
48	15 Sep '69 15 Sep '69	Port Discovery	S. L. Mastick 350 M ft. lumber 50 spars 50 M ft. piles	fresh SE gales; light NW pass.: B.S. Pettygrove, J. Keymes, R. Caimes, C. Brown, H. Reed, G. Chase
49[b]	7 Dec '69 7 Feb '70	Port Townsend	S. L. Mastick 300 M ft. lumber 1 M ft. spars 13 M ft. piles	strong SE; light NW pass.: Dr. Philips & wife
50	15 Feb '70 12 May '70	Port Townsend	S. L. Mastick 550 M ft.lumber 180 M laths 300 sks. potatoes.	hvy S gales, NW winds pass.: F. W. Pettygrove, wife & boy; Mrs. McKinlaw, E. Maloney
51	15 May '70 12 Jul '70	Port Townsend Port Discovery	S. L. Mastick 280 M ft. lumber 40 M laths 20 M ft. piles	light NW winds pass.: Mrs. Eisenbries Capt. F. W. Beck E. Murray

[a] Bill in Kentfield Papers 91/5.
[b] *Daily Alta California*, 30 Dec 1869.

Voyage	Departure Arrival	Ports of Call	Consignee/Cargo	Memoranda
52[a]	20 Jul '70 21 Sep '70	Port Discovery	S. L. Mastick 275 M Ft. lumber 22 M ft. piles 15 M laths 75 cans oil	
53	3 Oct '70 20 Nov '70	Port Discovery	S. L. Mastick 520 M ft. lumber 190 M laths	
54	26 Nov '70 9 Jan '71	Port Discovery	S. L. Mastick 315 M ft. lumber 160 M laths 100 T potatoes	strong s'ly; light n'ly pass.: Mr. Thebrick & dau., F. Gordon, S. A. Bent, J. Harvey
55	14 Jan '71 27 Feb '71	Port Townsend Port Discovery	S. L. Mastick 315 M ft. lumber 150 M laths 50 ships' knees	
56	12 Mar '71 18 Apr '71	Port Discovery	S. L. Mastick lumber, laths, potatoes	variable winds, rain
57	28 Apr '71 7 Jul '71	Port Discovery	S. L. Mastick 30 M ft. piles	fresh NW; lt SE & thick pass.: B. S. Pettygrove & sister
58[b]	16 Jul '71 2 Sep '71	Port Discovery	S. L. Mastick 550 M ft. lumber 180 M laths	NW winds all passage pass: Mrs. E. E. T. Wood and 2 children
59	21 Sep '71 18 Oct '71	Port Discovery	S. L. Mastick lumber	
60	29 Oct '71 22 Dec '71	Port Discovery	S. L. Mastick 530 M ft. lumber 180 M laths	
61	7 Jan '72 12 Feb '72	Port Discovery	S. L. Mastick 506,347 ft. lbr. (hold) 32,125 ft. lbr. (deck)	mod & reliable weather

[a] *Daily Alta California*, 10 Sep 1870.
[b] Mrs. Wood's husband was a partner in the S. L. Mastick Lumber Company.

Voyage	Departure Arrival	Ports of Call	Consignee/Cargo	Memoranda
62	23 Feb '72 2 Apr '72	Port Discovery	S. L. Mastick 540 M ft. lumber 80 M laths 5 T potatoes 2 bxs axes	
63[a]	11 Apr '72 3 Jun '72	Port Townsend Port Discovery	S. L. Mastick 17 M ft. piles	fresh SE gales; n'ly; light winds and calms 4-9 Jun, East St. Wharf
64	10 Jun '72 28 Jul '72	Port Townsend Nanaimo Race Rocks; Nanaimo	Mastick/Rosenfeld 1,200 T coal	calm and light winds; fresh NW
65	9 Aug '72 3 Oct '72	Port Discovery	S. L. Mastick 540 M ft. lumber 80 M wool slats	pass.: James M. Armour from Seabeck 5-9 Oct, East St. Wharf
66	15 Oct '72 23 Nov '72	Port Discovery Protection Is.	S. L. Mastick 540 M ft. lumber 180 M laths	fresh NE; variable; light SW and thick weather 25 Nov-3 Dec, East St. Wharf
67	3 Dec '72 13 Jan '73	Port Discovery	S. L. Mastick 550 M ft. lumber 1,020 M laths	15-21 Jan, East St. Wharf
68	21 Jan '73 13 Mar '73	Dungeness Port Discovery	S. L. Mastick: 530 M ft. lumber 150 M laths 30 T potatoes 21 M wool slats J. D. Wickham: 1 bale bear, dear & coon skins 8 rolls Indian matting	15-19 Mar, East St. Wharf
69[b]	22 Mar '73 21 Apr '73	Port Discovery	S. L. Mastick 550 M ft.lumber 190 laths	24-30 Apr, East St. Wharf

[a] Permanent register #63, issued at San Francisco 10 Apr 1872, surrendered 7 Aug 1872, lists Henry Revell as master (National Archives, RG 41). In 1868 he had been captain of the coaster *Rival* (*Lewis & Dryden*, 165).

[b] Possibly Capt. T. R. Arey of Port Hadlock, Washington Territory, who "began sailing in the coasting trade in 1865" (*Lewis & Dryden*, 459). The name appears in the 1850s in the shipbuilding firm of James Arey & Co., Frankfurt, Maine (William A. Fairburn, *Merchant Sail* [6 vols., repr. Gloucester, Massachusetts, 1992], v.3, *passim*).

Voyage	Departure Arrival	Ports of Call	Consignee/Cargo	Memoranda
70	1 May '73 25 Jun '73	Port Discovery Cape Flattery	S. L. Mastick 550 M ft. lumber 120 M laths 22 hides	hvy SE weather & rain most of the voyage
71	14 Jul '73 1 Dec '73	Port Discovery San Diego	S. L. Mastick 550 M ft. lumber 100 M laths 150 ships' knees	light NE; SE & SW winds, with heavy rains 2-8 Dec, East St. Wharf
72[a]	15 Dec '73 29 Jan '74	Port Discovery	S. L. Mastick 550 M ft. lumber 150 M laths	strong NW; SE winds 31 Jan-5 Feb, East St. Wharf
73[b]	6 Feb '74 20 Mar '74	Port Discovery	S. L. Mastick 580 M ft. lumber 75 M laths 14 M ft. piles potatoes	moderate NW pass.: Richard Jones 21-26 Mar, East St. Wharf
74	28 Mar '74 8 May '74	Port Discovery	S. L. Mastick 520 M ft. lumber 80 M laths 20 T potatoes	light winds and calm pass.: A. Newman, wife & child, Mrs. Pink, Miss Fraser, W. Scott 9-15 May, E. St. Wharf
75	15 May '74 21 Jun '74	Port Discovery	S. L. Mastick 240 M ft. lumber 200 M laths 17 M ft. piles	light SW; fresh SE last hours; pass.: Mrs. Pettygrove, Miss M. Roberts 22-27 Jun, E. St. Wharf
76	28 Jun '74 5 Aug '74	Port Discovery Dungeness Spit	S. L. Mastick 530 M ft. lumber	S & calm; light NW 6-11 Aug, E. St. Wharf
77	12 Aug '74 21 Sep '74	Port Discovery	S. L. Mastick 475 M ft. lumber 268 M laths	23-30 Sep, E. St. Wharf
78	21 Oct '74 11 Dec '74	Port Discovery	S. L. Mastick 223 M ft. lumber, 258 M laths 17 M ft. piles,14 T potatoes	

[a] Permanent enrollment #127 (8 Dec 1873) supersedes Port Townsend temporary register of 2 Aug 1873 (National Archives, RG 41 San Francsico).
[b] The "specification of cargo," dated at Port Discovery, March 12, 1874, lists 44 different lengths of lumber: 241,704 ft. under deck, 38,766 ft. on deck, including 80,000 laths.

Voyage	Departure Arrival	Ports of Call	Consignee/Cargo	Memoranda
79[a]	23 Dec '74 23 Feb '75	Port Discovery	S. L. Mastick 130 M ft. lumber 12 M laths 17,594 ft. piles	light, variable, fresh NW 23-27 Feb, E. St. Wharf
80[b]	28 Feb '75 24 Apr '75	Port Discovery	S. L. Mastick: 231 M ft. lumber 100 M ft. laths, 278 piles Conner: 373 sks potatoes	
81[c]	29 Apr '75 2 Jun '75	Port Discovery	S. L. Mastick 462 M ft. lumber 88 M laths	3-9 Jun, E. St. Wharf
82	10 Jun '75 10 Jul '75	Port Discovery	S. L. Mastick 469 M ft. lumber 88 M laths	
83	7 Aug '75 11 Sep '75	Port Discovery	S. L. Mastick lumber	300T ballast from S. F. 13-17 Sep, E. St. Wharf
84	18 Sep '75 28 Oct '75	Port Discovery	S. L. Mastick 500 M ft. lumber 270 M laths	29 Oct-5 Nov, East St. Wharf
85	6 Nov '75 21 Dec '75	Port Townsend Nanaimo Departure Bay	Berryman & Doyle 1,092 T coal	
86	2 Jan '76 21 Feb '76	Port Townsend Nanaimo Port Discovery	Berryman & Doyle 1,200 T coal	250T ballast from S. F.
87	6 Mar '76 3 May '76	Nanaimo Race Rocks	Berryman & Doyle 1,200 T coal	250 T ballast from S. F.
88	13 May '76 25 Jun '76	Nanaimo	Berryman & Doyle 1,200 T coal	7-15 Jul, Pacific St. Wharf Crew boarded at Union House, S.F., 10 Jul

[a] *Daily Alta California*, 24 Feb 1875.
[b] A new "topsail yard 14 in" was made on board at East Street Wharf; bill for $26. from Castner, Dale & Co. (Kentfield Papers 92/1). Conner's potatoes were shipped at a charge of $5 per ton.
[c] 17,713 ft. of Mastick's lumber fetched 15¢ a foot (WA 22 May 1875).

Voyage	Departure Arrival	Ports of Call	Consignee/Cargo	Memoranda
89	15 Jul '76 27 Aug '76	Port Townsend Nanaimo	Berryman & Doyle 1,250 T "merchantable coal"	29 Aug-8 Sep, Pacific St. Wharf
90	7 Sep '76 28 Oct '76	Nanaimo	Berryman & Doyle 1,250T coal	250T ballast from S. F. 29 Oct.-11 Nov, Pacific St. Wharf
91[a]	9 Nov '76 28 Dec '76	Nanaimo	Rosenfeld 1,225 T coal	
92[b]	8 Jan '77 23 Feb '77	Nanaimo	Berryman & Doyle 1,200 T coal	
93	10 Mar '77 7 Apr '77	Port Townsend Seattle	Rosenfeld 1,225 T coal	
94	18 Apr '77 6 Jun '77	Port Townsend Port Discovery	Kentfield/Mastick 270 M ft. lumber 250 M laths 18 M ft. piles	
95	10 Jun '77 17 Jul '77	Departure Bay	Berryman & Doyle 1,250 T coal	fresh NW; light SE and fogs
96	8 Aug '77 15 Sep '77	Port Townsend Nanaimo	Berryman & Doyle 1,250 T coal	outward: 1 pump, val. $450
97	12 Oct '77 21 Nov '77	Nanaimo	Berryman & Doyle 1,225 T coal	27 Nov-1 Dec, Oakland City Wharf
98	3 Dec '77 2 Jan '78	Port Townsend Departure Bay Nanaimo	Berryman & Doyle 1,210 T coal	9-23 Jan, Pacific St. Wharf
99	23 Jan '78 7 Mar '78	Departure Bay Port Townsend	Berryman & Doyle 1,210 T coal	strong SE & SW gales 7-15 Mar, Pacific St. Wharf

[a] Tonnage duties paid by Rosenfeld, 29 Dec 1876 (National Archives, San Bruno, "Record of Tonnage Duties").

[b] Capt. Hinds, born in Maine in 1825, had been master of whaling vessels in the Arctic and Pacific oceans for twelve years before coming to San Francisco ca. 1864 (Hittell, *Commerce*, 142).

Voyage	Departure Arrival	Ports of Call	Consignee/Cargo	Memoranda
100[a]	15 Mar '78 17 Apr '78	Departure Bay Port Townsend	Berryman & Doyle 1,220 T coal	250T ballast outward In the straits, heavy w'ly, since, mod NW
101	1 May '78 11 Jun '78	Port Townsend Port Discovery Nanaimo Race Rocks	Kentfield/Berryman & Doyle 1,230 T coal	250T ballast From S. F. 13-20 Jun, Pacific St. Wharf
102	20 Jun '78 1 Aug '78	Nanaimo	Berryman & Doyle 1,250 T coal	250T ballast from S. F. 23-27 Aug, Vallejo Wf 27-29 Aug, Oakland Wf 2 Sep, to Green St. Wf
103[b]	4 Sep '78 23 Oct '78	Departure Bay	Dunsmuir & Diggle 1,225 coal	24-29 Oct, Pacific St. Wharf to Beale St. Mer- chant's Dry Dock, Green St. Wharf
104	9 Nov '78 19 Dec '78	Departure Bay Race Rocks	Dunsmuir & Diggle 1,180 T coal	strong SE gales, light northerly weather 25 Dec-4 Jan, Pacific St. Wharf
105	4 Jan '79 30 Mar '79	Wellington Esquimalt Nanaimo Departure Bay	Dunsmuir & Diggle 1,200 T coal	250T ballast from S. F. 31 Mar-11 Apr, Pacific St. Wharf
106	12 Apr '79 26 May '79	Departure Bay	Dunsmuir & Diggle 1,210 T coal	250T ballast from S. F. 26 May-14 Jun, Pacific St. Wharf
107	14 Jun '79 8 Aug '79	Departure Bay	Dunsmuir & Diggle 1,235 T coal	

[a] *Daily Alta California*, 10 Apr 1878.

[b] Kentfield Papers 93/1: bills from *Daily Alta California* and Guide Publishing Co. Dunsmuir & Diggle owned vast deposits of coal in Washington and Vancouver Island. The mines at Nanaimo possessed the most complete and convenient arrangements for extracting and shipping the coal. They were at a disadvantage, however, because of the heavy tariff, which cut off much of their profit in the American market. Their Wellington Colliery, at Departure Bay, three and a half miles north of Nanaimo, was opened in 1870. In 1882, when their price was usually $1-$2 more per ton than coal from Seattle, they sold about half their yield in San Francisco, the remainder in Wilmington (to the Southern Pacific Railway) and the Hawaiian Islands. The company owned two steamships and frequently chartered sailing vessels such as the *Revere* (Hittell, *Commerce*, 590,753,760,767,769,774,783).

Voyage	Departure Arrival	Ports of Call	Consignee/Cargo	Memoranda
108	21 Aug '79 29 Dec '79	Nanaimo Royal Roads Pillar Point Honolulu Departure Bay	Dunsmuir & Diggle 1,150 T coal	250T ballast from S. F. fresh N winds & snow; calms & light southerly weather 29 Dec-7 Jan, Pacific St. Wharf
109	7 Jan '80 13 Feb '80	Departure Bay	Dunsmuir & Diggle 1,180 T coal	calms, fresh NW winds 13-27 Feb, Pacific St. Wharf discharging coal
110ᵃ	27 Feb '80 3 Apr '80	Departure Bay	Dunsmuir & Diggle 1,250 T coal	southerly winds & rain 9-17 Apr, Pacific St. Wf
111	19 Apr '80 28 May '80	Victoria Departure Bay	Dunsmuir & Diggle 1,100 T coal	
112ᵇ	12 Jun '80 15 Feb '81	Nanaimo Honolulu Port Townsend	Dunsmuir & Diggle coal	
113	2 Mar '81 1 Apr '81	Port Townsend	Kentfield/Seattle Coal & Tr. Co. 1,178 T coal	
114ᶜ	22 Apr '81 13 Aug '81	Seabeck San Diego	W. J. Adams 305 M ft. lumber 1,080 piles	

ᵃ Tonnage duties collected from J. Kentfield & Co. (NA, San Bruno, "Record of tonnage duties.").
ᵇ *Daily Alta California*, 10 Jun 1880; shipping articles, Kentfield Papers 93/6.
ᶜ NA, RG 41 San Francsico. Wm. J. Adams, a lumber manufacturer and shipping merchant, had officers at 17 Stewart St (Hittell, *Commerce*, 767, 783).

(Continued from page 84)

building the Texas and Pacific Railway, and that she return to Port Discovery to reload for San Francisco.[11]

A short turnaround time was essential to profitability, and Captain McIntyre averaged about six voyages annually. The *Puget Sound Weekly Argus* complimented him on having taken only twenty-eight days from Port Discovery to San Francisco and back—"remarkably quick time," they observed. Too quickly, perhaps, for a week later, the *Revere* found herself ashore on Dungeness Spit [voyage 76] though she was apparently gotten off in a few hours, unharmed.[12] Thomas J. Conner, mate a year earlier under McIntyre's command, took over as master in September 1874 on the return voyage from Port Discovery [voyage 77].[13] At about the same time, the period of economic depression ended, at least temporarily, and he was able to continue the regular runs of his predecessor.

After the *Revere*'s return to San Francisco in July 1875 [voyage 82], she underwent substantial changes to convert her rig from ship to bark. The largest single item of expense was for ship chandlery: $3,829.28 due G. M. Josselyn & Co. The bill from William Bell, carpenter, totalled $1,808.67, and from William Simmons, rigger, $450, for "heaving down" the ship and altering her rig. Over and above this $6,000 expenditure, lesser amounts were owed to sundry local contractors:[14]

C. H. Currier, pump and block maker, 28 Market
W. M. Hendry & Co., ship and steamboat smiths, 26 Folsom
Wm. Green, rigger and contractor, 26 Howard and 14 Spear
A. Crawford & Co., ship chandlers, 27, 29 Market
Stoffer & Mighell, dealers in new and second-hand ship
    materials, 5 Market
T. Taylor, ship painting and scraping
Harding and Brann, sailmakers, 54-56 Clay
Coombs & Taylor, shipwrights, caulkers, and spar makers, 107-
    109 Market
Pendergast & Smith, iron founders and machinists
Risdon Iron & Locomotive works, Beale & Howard
Charles Hare, old iron, copper & metal, 34-36 Stewart
California Mills, Howard & Spear
Adams, Blinn & Co., lumber dealers, 17 Stewart

G. A. Meigs, wholesale and retail lumber dealer, Pier 1,
        Stewart

The alterations seem not to have affected the city and county
assessments on the ship at San Francisco. For 1873-74 and 1874-75 the
figure had been $12,000—up from $8,000 in 1868-69; for 1875-76 it was
$7,000, where it stayed until 1879-80, after which the assessment de-
creased progressively to $4,500 in the disaster year, 1883-84.[15]

A few records of payments to shareowners during the first ten of
the Kentfield years survive, described as "acct. *Revere* in full of earnings
to date":

2 Oct. 1871	to Calvin Paige	$811.85
15 Mar. 1872	" "	594.34
"	Mastick	594.34
August 1873	Mastick	120.40
22 May 1874	C. Paige	428.00

and, for the year 1876, cancelled checks testify to payments to Mastick
as part-owner:

17 Mar.	on acct. earnings	$500.00
31 "	balance *Revere* earnings t.d. 242.66	
19 May	in full--earnings to date	515.84
16 Sept.	in full for 1/3 earnings to date	527.63
24 Nov.	in full for 1/3 near earnings	
	bk. *Revere* trip ending Nov.76	614.70

Assuming that the first two payments represented earnings on
the 2 January-21 February [voyage 86] and that the other payments applied to the next four voyages [numbers 87-90], a reasonable estimate for
the total return on the year's six voyages would be $2,881 to each of the
three owners. Hypothetical as this figure may be, it is interesting to note
that in a single three-week period in port [voyage 98], with no major
outlays beyond the cost of discharging a cargo of coal ($423.60) and
presumably no wages to be paid to captain or crew, the bills for normal

repairs and provisioning totalled about $650, plus another $187.50 for 250 tons of ballast—all together somewhat more than one dollar of expense chargeable to each ton of the 1,210-ton loads of coal shipped.[16] In this same period the bottom dropped out of the lumber trade, so that mills kept little stock on hand and sawed to order. The Kentfield owners profited more by shipping for coal merchants.

In November 1875 [voyage 85] Berryman & Doyle became the regular consignee,[17] for whom 1,200-1,250 tons of "merchantable coal" were shipped at approximately two-month intervals from Dunsmuir, Diggle's Wellington colliery at Departure Bay, British Columbia. Captain McIntyre took over from Conner once again in May 1876 for the return [voyage 87], reportedly having purchased an interest in the *Revere*.[18] The information was, however, some four years premature. Calvin Paige was still receiving his share of the profits,[19] and Kentfield's son had not yet acquired Levi Mastick's share of ownership.

Berryman & Doyle disappear as consignees after the June 1878 voyage from San Francisco [number 102], and on 2 September the *Daily Alta California* advertised the services of the *Revere*: "For Victoria and Nanaimo, B.C. The Bark *Revere*, McINTYRE . . . Master, will receive freight for the above ports on Tuesday, Sept. 3, and will have quick dispatch. For freight apply to A. Packscher, 423 Jackson Street."

The advertisement paid off with Packscher shipping a cargo valued at $3,767 to Victoria, British Columbia [voyage 103]:[20] a variety of hardware supplies, furniture, staple foods, and three stoves (table 16).

Receipt issued by S. L. Mastick for payment from the *Revere* account. Courtesy, Bancroft Library.

The gains were short-lived, however. When the *Revere* next cleared San Francisco [voyage 104] her only cargo consisted of twelve kegs of nails valued at $39.[21] For the return voyage Dunsmuir, Diggle & Co. was consignee and became a regular, though perhaps less predictable customer than some of its predecessors. On the next voyage [number 105] the captain brought troubles on his own head, having fallen into disfavor with the Nanaimo port authorities by dumping ballast "in Departure Bay not in the place set apart by the harbor master for that purpose."[22]

On the voyage departing in mid-April 1879 [number 106] there was some doubt as to the prospects for finding a load with reasonable dispatch at Departure Bay. Kentfield wired the firm of Welch, Rithet & Co. at Victoria to keep watch for the *Revere* and instruct her to go to Port Blakely. Similar telegrams were sent to the captain, c/o Welch, Rithet, but he was already at Departure Bay, where he eventually picked up 1,210 tons of coal "more or less" for the account of Dunsmuir, Diggle.[23] Uncertainty prevailed likewise as to cargo for the subsequent voyage [number 107], which departed 14 June 1879 from San Francisco to Departure Bay. If the ship had not already sailed from British Columbia, Welch, Rithet were to instruct the captain to send her to Wilmington, which was being developed as the harbor for Los Angeles. But it was too late. She already had a cargo of 1,195.85 tons of coal, plus 426.81 tons of oak in 1/2 ft. lengths, from Wellington Colliery for Dunsmuir, Diggle in San Francisco.[24]

Having chartered the *Revere* as collier for five consecutive coastwise passages, Dunsmuir, Diggle decided to seek a new market. Captain McIntyre was to take the ship to Nanaimo [voyage 108], to load coal for Honolulu.[25] The 1,228 tons consigned to him was shipped from their Wellington Mine at a cost to Dunsmuir, Diggle of $3,750. In Honolulu, where the *Revere* entered on 28 October 1879, it was delivered to the account of H. Hackfeld & Co.*, at $7.625 per ton. After deducting their commission of 5 percent plus guarantee ($468.17) and the $2.50

---

* This old German trading firm began importing lumber into Hawaii in 1849 and expanded into other commodities. Eventually going into sugar exporting, they became well-established and influential. The company survives today as the wholly-owned American company, Amfac, Ltd.

customs entry fee, Hackfeld would owe the Kentfield *Revere* account $8,892.83, payable at San Francisco within ninety days. The ship returned to Nanaimo in ballast.

From January through May 1880 [voyages 109-111] Captain McIntyre bettered his own time-average on coastwise passages for Dunsmuir, Diggle. But the Sandwich Islands—and their demand for coal—beckoned. Early in June, after her cargo had been discharged, the *Revere* was towed from Merchants' Dry Dock (pres., Oliver Eldridge) to Cousins' Dry Dock for cleaning and repairs. Her shipping articles stipulated that Captain McIntyre sail her from San Francisco to Nanaimo, thence to the Sandwich Islands with a load of coal, and from there to any port or ports in the North or South Pacific Ocean—the voyage [number 112] not to exceed twelve months.[26] At Main Street Wharf she took on water and ballast, and was piloted out of San Francisco harbor on 12 June, consigned to Dunsmuir, Diggle. At Departure Bay, where she put

Table 16. Voyage 103 cargo: San Francisco to Victoria

Product	Amount
barley (ground)	50 sacks
bran	147 sacks
brooms	5 doz.
case goods	10 cs
coal oil	425 cs
flour	400 qtr sks
furniture	8 pkgs
hams	3 tcs
hardware	3 pkgs
machinery	8 pkgs
malt	235 sks
meal	32 sks
oakum	9 bbls
pumps	2
rosin	10 bbls
stoves	3
woodenware	37 pkgs

Source: Daily Alta California, 6 Sep 1878.

in on 5 July, she loaded 1,211 tons of coal for Hackfeld & Co. in Honolulu. The cargo, valued there at $3,663, was discharged between 31 July and 18 August. By 20 September the *Revere* was back in Puget Sound—at Port Townsend, and then at Departure Bay, now loading for Wilmington, after a voyage of considerably less than the allotted twelve months. There she discharged coal, took on ballast and shipped new crew, and on 27 October sailed again for Port Townsend, Washington Territory. On 24 November she was towed from Sail Rock to Race Rock, en route to Wellington Colliery for another cargo of coal, to be delivered at San Francisco for Dunsmuir, Diggle.[27]

Neither the Honolulu nor the Wilmington route had conformed to the usual *Revere* schedule, and the events of the month that followed were even more out of the ordinary. As Captain McIntyre reported at a later date:[28]

The Bark *"Revere"* under my command sailed from Departure Bay, B.C. on or about the 3rd of December 1880, laden with coal and bound for San Francisco. At 6 P.M. of same day came to anchor in Esquimalt Harbor, filled up water and at 10^{30} P.M. proceeded on our intended voyage, with strong N.N.E. winds and thick snow storm.

Decr. 4th. Continued with wind & weather the same at noon. Cape Flattery bore N.N.E. distant 25 miles.

Decr. 6th at 8 P.M. strong southerly wind with squalls and heavy cross sea, ship making more water than usual. . . . At 11 P.M. found the water gaining, got steam up on donkey engine and hooked on both pumps. At 1 A.M. 5 feet water in well. At 7 A.M. got water down to 20 inches, ship leaking 18 inches per hour. Threw overboard about 30 tons of coal and then put on hatches; much water coming on board. Engine running most of the time.

Decr. 8th. Leak continuing the same & donkey engine using salt water and leaking; concluded to bear up for Esquimalt for the general preservation. Threw overboard about 20 tons of coal. Weather continuing stormy with heavy sea, ship leaking the same.

Decr. 12 at 10 P.M. in a heavy squall split Foresail and Upper Foretopsail. At 9 A.M. came to anchor in Esquimalt, ship still making the same quantity of water.

The situation was desperate, even for a captain with more than fifteen years at sea. He wired both Kentfield and Rosenfeld from Port Townsend on 13 December: "Returned Esquimalt leaking very badly. Leak must be in garboard. Must discharge cargo. Wish you would come or send Edwards. I am unable to be round, having been disabled by donkey engine." The reply—as immediate as the telegraph system of the day could deliver: "Can't you get diver to go down and find leak, if not, you will have to discharge to repair. . . . I will send Murray carpenter up if you think best." But there was no diver. McIntyre decided that the ship should go to Departure Bay with George M. T. White in charge.[29] He himself would be on hand as soon as he could get out of bed. But—urgently—"send Murray!"

Kentfield postponed any further instructions until he had seen Diggle, to whom the 1,165 tons of coal was consigned. Then the advice from San Francisco on 14 December was to go back to Departure Bay and discharge into some other vessel or, if need be, to beach the ship and repair her on land. Another day, another tactic; the wire the following day instructed: if the *Revere* is still at Esquimalt, keep her there pending possible sale of the cargo there. On 16 December the orders were changed again, to deliver it to Welch, Rithet, to land part at Esquimalt and the balance at Victoria. The good news was, "Mr. Murray and Litter on steamer."

The ship remained in Esquimalt until December 29, discharging coal, and was then towed to Victoria, "not leaking so badly." When discharging was suspended, there were still about 250 tons on board for ballast. On January 1 she was towed to sea and proceeded toward Port Townsend, arriving on the second, where she was again enrolled to engage in the "coasting trade." Then, according to McIntyre: "Jany 4th towed to Port Blakely. 4th, commenced discharging coal—7th, completed discharging. 10th, hauled ship on beach and listed her over, but the tide did not fall low enough to find the leak. 11th, At low water found the leak in garboard seam, water running out freely, stopped the leak and patched the copper. 12th, hauled vessel off and commenced to take in [217-1/2T] coal for Dunsmuir and Diggle."

Finally, on the twenty-second she was at Utsalady, Washington Territory, where 495,584 feet of white pine and 113M laths were loaded from the Puget Sound Mill Co., consigned to Pope & Talbot, lumber dealers in San Francisco. They owned not only the mill and the Victoria & Puget Sound Packets, but also two mills at Port Gamble and one at Port Ludlow; in addition, as the Puget Sound Commercial Company, the firm had some sixteen vessels of their own, measuring 14.5 thousand tons in the aggregate.[30]

Captain McIntyre was now sufficiently recovered to take back his command from George White. In contrast to her voyages of earlier years, the *Revere* was now employed in a new trade of hauling lumber, where deck-loads were accepted, required and common. On 28 January 1881 they finished taking on cargo, including a load on deck, proceeded on the thirtieth to Port Townsend, and on February first to sea, bound for San Francisco, where they arrived two weeks later. Then the calculations of general average could begin, so that the expense of the disaster would be shared by owners of ship and cargo proportionately. The detailed statements of disbursements, cargo and freight jettisoned, wages and provisions for the vessel's company, contributory interest and apportionment, all allocated between "first general average" and owners, were then submitted to an adjuster for settlement (*see* appendix C.2):[31]

> *In re Bark "Revere"*
>
> Messrs. Hutchinson Mann, agents of insurers on cargo, and Capt. [*sic*] Jno. Kentfield, owner of the "Revere," have agreed to leave out to Messrs. C. V. S. Gibbs and C. T. Hopkins the question as to the liability of insurers on cargo (who had become owners thereof by the acceptance of an abandonment) to pro rata freight on that portion of the cargo which was voluntarily accepted at Esquimalt on the vessel's way from Departure Bay to San Francisco.
>
> The undersigned decides the claim in favor of the ship (Mr. Gibbs declining to concur) on the authority of Phillips #1634 . . . [and page] 345, vol. 2. . . . See also Sec. 1988, same authority—#434 et seq. . . . The question is also fully discussed in Th. Parsons on Maritime Law, p. 165, and notes thereto.
>
> The only question remaining is as to the amount the *Revere* is entitled to charge for freight *pro rata itineris* in the present case. The

whole freight to be earned from Departure Bay to San Francisco was $4. per ton. The regular coasting rate on coal from Departure Bay to Victoria was $1.50 at the time in question.

Nothing could have been realized by the *Revere* by procuring another vessel to have brought on the cargo from Victoria or Esquimalt, for as far as appears the *Revere* was chartered for several voyages at $4., while owing to a rise in freights during the time occupied by the voyage, probably $6. would have been demanded to complete the voyage in question.

I find no absolute rule in the books for estimating the *quantum meruit* in such cases, but in view of all the circumstances I believe that 50¢ per ton is a fair compromise valuation of the service performed in the present case.

[*signed*] C. Thos. Hopkins

By 24 February 1881 the coal and lumber had been discharged at the Main Street Wharf, San Francisco. The *Revere* was then briefly at Merchants' Dry Dock for coppering—not in the usual fashion but with Cape Ann, Massachusetts, copper paint—caulking, and carpentry. She took on ballast and water and on 2 March was towed to sea, bound for Port Townsend [voyage 113], with McIntyre in command and Kentfield as agent. On arrival, the master dutifully secured permission to discharge ballast at Yesler's Wharf for a ten-day period. The new consignee was the Seattle Coal and Transportation Company, with offices in San Francisco. Their shipment of coarse and nut coal, totalling 1,178.09 tons, arrived in port on April 11, twenty-one days from Seattle, in southeast winds and gale.[32]

New shipping articles ordered McIntyre to load for San Diego, thence to Puget Sound to load for any port in the North or South Pacific [voyage 114]—San Francisco to be a final port of discharge within twelve months. The voyage, however, was only coastwise: to Seabeck at the north end of the Hood Canal where the Washington Mill was located (12-29 May), Port Townsend (towage down Strait of Juan de Fuca, 30 May), San Diego and National City (12-28 June), and back to Port Townsend and Seabeck (18 July-3 Aug) At the Washington Mill she loaded on deck 52,993 ft. rough lumber, under deck 252,381 more, in addition to 1,080 piles (21,646 ft.)—all consigned to W. J. Adams in San Francisco, with the possible addition of 200,000 laths, if the news report is accurate.[33]

Before the *Revere* even reached San Francisco a new charter, dated 13 August 1881, had been drawn up between John Kentfield, agent for her owners, and Williams, Dimond & Co., also of San Francisco.[34] The contract provided for the

> freighting and chartering of the whole of the said vessel [with the exception of the deck, cabin and the necessary room for the crew, and the stowage of provisions, sails, and cables, or sufficient room for the cargo] for a voyage from Departure Bay, B.C., to Honolulu, H.I. . . . This vessel shall proceed from this port (S.F.) in ballast to Departure Bay, B.C., with all possible dispatch . . . [Williams, Dimond to] provide and furnish to the said vessel a full and complete cargo of coal or so much as the vessel can safely stow and carry. The cargo to be furnished at Departure Bay, B.C., by Messrs. Dunsmuir, Diggle & Co. (Wellington Colliery), the vessel to take her regular turn in loading and with despatch according to the custom of the port, and to pay . . . five dollars and fifty cents ($5.50) U.S. gold coin for each and every ton of 2240 lbs. gross weight delivered at Honolulu. Freight payable here (S.F.) by charterers on return of the proper documents. Vessel to dunnage sufficient for the proper care of the cargo, to employ stevedore satisfactory to charterers, and to be stowed under the Captain's supervision and direction. The Captain to sign bills of lading as desired by charterers . . . but at no less than chartered rates. . . . The lay days for loading and discharging shall . . . commence twenty-four hours after the . . . Captain has notified [the charterers] that the vessel is ready to receive or discharge cargo. . . . And for each and every day's detention (beyond as above) by default of said parties of the second part, or their agents, fifty dollars ($50) per day, day by day, shall be paid . . . to said parties of the first part. . . . Commissions at San Francisco five (5%) per cent on estimated amount of this charter payable to Williams, Dimond & Co. . . . by the vessel before clearing [at San Francisco].

5

BETWEEN PUGET SOUND AND THE SANDWICH ISLANDS

1881-1883

Having been cleared at San Francisco on 26 August 1881 for a voyage not to exceed twelve months [number 115; *see* table 17 for details of subsequent voyages], the *Revere* reached Nanaimo on 4 September to take on 1,200 tons of coal and 2,800 pounds of potatoes consigned to her master.[1] She sailed on 20 September for Honolulu, where her cargo, valued at $3,700, was discharged quickly and ballast loaded for the return voyage. On 8 November, while she was under way to Royal Roads [Esquimalt] for orders, a new charter party, [voyage 116] was negotiated with Allen & Robinson of Honolulu.[2]

The terms were similar to those of the previous contract, except for a new clause providing that "so much of said freight as the Capt. may require for the vessel's disbursements at Honolulu to be paid to him there by charterers free of charge, the balance . . . by a draft on San Francisco free of exchange, the draft to be payable sixty (60) days from date of delivery of cargo." The charterers also were protected by a new provision that freight "be paid on invoice quantity unless any of the cargo is jettisoned; in that case on the output." The charterer's previous experience with contributory interest and general averages had been instructive.

The insurance policy issued to Kentfield for the ensuing year (1 Dec 1881-1 Dec 1882) covered the "body tackle, apparel, and other furniture of the ship," valuation $10,000, with $2,000 to be paid in case of loss during that period. An endorsement guaranteed that the firm would "pay 1 per cent, additional premiums for each trip to Nanaimo or Departure Bay, until 14% in all has been paid, thereafter privilege to use said ports without extra charge." The normal charge had been established at 11%, for a cost of $220 on the $2,000 policy.

The invoices for the Honolulu charters normally included towage charges in and out of Nanaimo or Port Townsend, and also at Honolulu; the Oahu police check on the day prior to departure; water and as much as 250 tons of stone ballast at Honolulu; "necessary disbursements" to the provisioners Waterman & Katz, or to Rothschild in Puget Sound; expenses in Honolulu, for which Allen & Robinson reimbursed the captain—eventually—crediting them against the final payment to Kentfield.

In the summer of 1882 the *Revere* was at Port Blakely and Port Townsend between 18 July and 8 August, loading lumber, reportedly for the Sandwich Islands. The local gazette was misinformed, or the orders changed, for the next shipping articles specified that voyage 119 be run from Port Townsend to San Francisco, where she entered on 24 August.[3] Captain McIntyre purchased Calvin Paige's shares just prior to a remeasurement of the vessel, which then received a new permanent register. Her capacity was now calculated at 762 88/100 "under the tonnage-deck" and 67 05/100 "of inclosures on upper deck," which would result in lower tonnage duties to be assessed at the end of the year.

The permanent register issued at San Francisco on 30 August 1882 was duly endorsed by the collector of the port at Port Townsend, district of Puget Sound, to provide for a change of master. Captain J. H. Hinds, who had taken over on one round-voyage to San Francisco in 1887 [*see* chapter 4, voyages 92-93], would take the *Revere* to Honolulu, returning to any port in the United States. On the previous occasion McIntyre had been reported in poor health on arrival at Nanaimo, where typhoid fever was epidemic. The Port Townsend newspaper, which followed the comings and goings of its favorite adopted son, had expressed the hope that "ere long the quarter deck of the good old bark will welcome his return with renewed health and vigor." Now, when Hinds took over for the second time, Captain McIntyre was reported simply as having stayed with his family in the city. In fact, he had made his final voyage as master of the *Revere*.

Another set of shipping articles, issued at San Francisco, specified a twelve-month limit on the extended return voyage to Honolulu via Port Blakely for loading in Puget Sound, and back to San Francisco. The *Revere* was cleared coastwise on 4 September without cargo, having taken on fifteen tons of ballast, plus stores of flour, china nut oil, security oil and fish oil. Four days out, one of the crewmen drowned after he jumped overboard "while crazed with drink." At Port Townsend on 5 October another set of shipping articles was issued, superseding the previous ones [voyage 120] but failing to specify the final port of discharge in the United States.[4]

Captain Hinds returned to Port Townsend on 13 June 1883 [voyage 122]—only seventeen days from Honolulu—with late Honolulu newspapers, but no passengers or cargo. On 16 July [voyage 123] a new cargo was loaded and new crew, ages 23 to 52, shipped.[5] Truly international in make-up, it included citizens of England (2), Queensland, Australia (1), Finland (3), Norway (3), Scotland (1), Sweden (2) and one lone American from Pensacola, Florida.[6] They arrived at Honolulu at midnight on 6 August—after twenty-one days en route, with fair weather and few calms. The local newspaper reported each day on the progress of discharging the cargo: 120,000 feet; only about 50,000 feet; "discharging from her lower hold"; about 75,000 feet—and so on, for the ten days needed to unload the laths and 600,000 feet of northwest lumber. On 22 August she was reported as the first vessel to have sailed for Port Townsend in some time.[7] She carried a crew of twelve, Captain Hinds, and four passengers: O. Hessler, F. Steuler, P. Frederic and son.

Having passed Cape Flattery and into the Strait of Juan de Fuca, at 5 A.M. on 9 September 1883, the *Revere* "drifted ashore in fog and

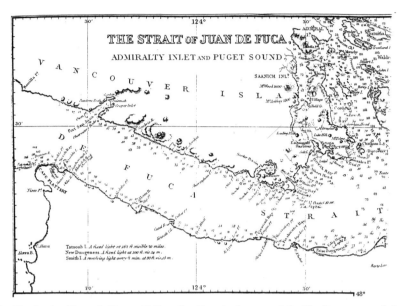

The Strait of Juan de Fuca with Port San Juan in the upper left. The *Revere* grounded just west of that harbor.

calm; no wind and thick fog; day light, no wind, heavy swell . . . one half mile west of San Juan Harbor, British Columbia." Both anchors were dropped "but owing to heavy swell vessel dragged on to Rocks," according to the wreck report signed by Captain Hinds. No assistance was rendered, no life lost, and there was no cargo aboard. The crew and passengers were brought to Victoria by the Indians the next day. The *Weekly Argus*, characteristically, viewed the disaster from the point of view of a long-time master, who "had worked long and hard to accumulate the property and must feel its loss greatly. . . . She was uninsured, though Capt. McIntyre's [one-third] interest carried a policy until quite recently. The many friends of Capt. McIntyre here deeply sympathize with the Captain in his loss." It remained only for Captain Hinds to pay off the crew and then, on 17 September, to surrender the certificate of registry at Port Townsend along with the formal wreck report. The value of the vessel was estimated at $15,000, of damage to the vessel: "total."[8]

Cat. No. 221.

WRECK REPORT.

[Under act June 20, 1874, and Treasury Circular No. 69.]

Puget Sound   Collection District.

1. Date, (hour of day, day of week, day of month, year.)	1.	9th day September 1883 at 5 oclock P.M.
2. Nationality, rig, and full name of vessel, (wood or iron.)	2.	American Bark Revere (wood)
3. Tonnage.	3.	795 47/100 two
4. Age.	4.	Thirty four Years
5. Port where registered.	5.	~~Honolulu S.I.~~ San Francisco Cla
6. Official number.	6.	21629
7. Name and residence of master.	7.	J.F. Hinds Port Townsend, Wash Terr
8. Name and residence of owner.	8.	E.C. John Rosenfield San Francisco Cla & J.F. Hinds Port Townsend WT
9. Port last sailed from and date of sailing.	9.	Honolulu H.S.I. August 20th 1883
10. Where bound.	10.	Port Townsend Wash Terr
11. Number of passengers.	11.	four
12. Number of crew, including masters, mates, &c.	12.	Thirteen
13. Number and names of persons lost.	13.	none
14. Estimated value of vessel.	14.	Fifteen Thousand Dollars
15. Estimated value of cargo.	15.	none
16. Nature of cargo.	16.	0 "
17. Had vessel a deck-load?	17.	0 "
18. Was she overladen?	18.	0 "
19. Weight of cargo.	19.	0 "
20. Estimated loss or damage to vessel.*	20.	Total
21. Estimated loss or damage to cargo.	21.	0
22. Amount of insurance on vessel.	22.	none
23. Amount of insurance on cargo.	23.	"
24. Locality of casualty. (giving precise point of land or other obstruction in case of stranding.)	24.	one half mile West John Jung Harbor B.C.
25. Nature of casualty, (whether foundering, stranding, or other disaster.†)	25.	Drifted ashore in Sluggy Calm
26. Cause of the casualty, (specifying particularly.)	26.	No Wind and Thick Fogg
27. Force of wind, state of weather and sea; if at night, whether moonlight, starlight, or dark.‡	27.	Daylight no wind heavy swell
28. By whom and to what extent assistance was rendered.	28.	none
29. State, in detail, measures taken to avoid casualty.	29.	Ancor droped but owing to heavy swell Vessel draged on to rocks
30. Remarks. (All particulars not included in the foregoing will be here stated.)	30.	

Pt Townsend WT   *Sept 12th* , 188*3*.

J. F. Hinds
Master Bark Revere

* Estimated total amount of loss is desired, without regard to what may be covered by insurance, and should be expressed in figures.
† In case of collision, the name and hailing port of the colliding vessel should be given if possible.
‡ Whether calm, gentle breeze, strong breeze, moderate gale, strong gale, storm, or hurricane.
§ The person making this report will sign his name as managing owner, agent, or master, as the case may be.

[Ed. 5-16-'82 5,000.]

Wreck report of the *Revere*, filed at Port Townsend, Washington Territory, Puget Sound District, Collector of Customs. National Archives, RG 36: Puget Sound District, Collector of Customs.

In all probability the loss to Kentfield was far less than the loss, both personal and financial, to Captain McIntyre. He was fortunate to have been off-duty on this occasion. Later, he was in command of the *Richard III* for six years and, from about 1889, of the steam collier *Bristol*—his first command in steam—running from Oyster Harbor, Washington Territory to Alaska. On 2 January 1902, laden with coal, she was driven ashore on the reefs of some small islands along the Inside Passage, not far from Prince Rupert. Two lifeboats, with twenty persons on board, reached shore, but Captain McIntyre and six of his crew were lost—the last load to leave the vessel, which sank as the seventy-year old captain stepped into the lifeboat.[9] In the end, though, it was still the *Revere* that had claimed his longest service—half of her life afloat, during which time he commanded more than eighty of her voyages.

The *Revere* served Kentfield & Co. well over a period of almost twenty years, and Howes & Crowell for nearly as long—an unusually long life for a sailing vessel. Surviving her share of disasters, she logged untold numbers of sea-miles in the course of her 123 voyages. Typical of a hard-working merchant ship, she carried cargo where it was needed, quietly, efficiently. Her nobility comes from her steadfastness—she was always there and always performed when and as needed. Today, through the many documents of her recorded history, she provides a window to nineteenth-century seafaring America.

EPILOGUE

There now appears to be a remote possibility that the window to nineteenth-century seafaring America provided by the *Revere* history may be opened just a notch further if the current survey project of the Department of Canadian Heritage continues to yield artifacts. James Ringer, the marine archeologist for the project, has reported to Captain Huycke the recovery of a brass gudgeon and pintle near Owen Point, in the Port San Juan harbor area. He notes, however, that the finds might in fact be from another vessel, the *William Tell*, which likewise met its fate in the vicinity at approximately the same time.

M.R.G.

Table 17. Voyages 115-123

Note: All dates of departure and arrival are from Puget Sound.

Voyage	Departure Arrival	Ports of Call	Consignee/Cargo	Memoranda
115	26 Aug '81 26 Nov '81	Nanaimo Honolulu	Williams, Dimond 1,200T coal	In ballast return in ballast
116	Dec '81 31 Jan '82	Honolulu	Allen & Robinson 1,180 T coal val. $3,540	return in ballast
117	11 Feb '82 8 Apr '82	Honolulu	Allen & Robinson 1,180T coal val $3,540	return in ballast pass.: James Maxwell to Nanaimo
118	8 May '82 15 Jul '82	Honolulu	Allen & Robinson coal: val. $3,692	pass.: C. F. Rostedt to Pt. Townsend
119	8 Aug '82 15 Sep '82	Pt. Madison Pt. Townsend	E. M. Herrick 575M ft. lbr. 55M laths	
120	6 Oct '82 18 Dec '82	Pt. Blakeley Honolulu	Allen & Robinson rough lumber, 150M ft ($5,016) dressed lbr., 40M ($3,000) laths ($80)—total value $8,096	return in ballast
121	2 Jan '83 20 Mar '83	Honolulu	Allen & Robinson lbr: value $3,405	pass.: M McInness fare to Pt. Townsend $40
122	6 Apr '83 13 Jun	Honolulu	Allen & Robinson 496,594 ft. lbr. 85,308 do. 10M cedar shingles 6,667 laths (total 598,569 ft.) val. $7,715.30	return in ballast pass.: Mrs. G. West & child
123	16 Jul '83 [see text]	Honolulu	Allen & Robinson 466, 900 ft rough NW lbr. 132,315 ft. surface NW lbr. 100M shingles/val. $4,684.79	pass.: [see text]

Sources: *Daily Alta California*; Kentfield Papers.

APPENDICES
END NOTES
ABOUT THE AUTHOR
BIBLIOGRAPHY
INDEX

APPENDIX A
HOWES' RIG

The size of the crew on a sailing ship was partly dictated by the size of the sails the ship carried. Canvas was heavy and the larger a sail, the more men were required to furl or stow it. Ships of the pre-clipper era had relatively large sails and proportionally large crews. As steamships became more common on the ocean highways, sailing ship masters looked for ways to become more competitive. The obvious thing was to reduce expenses. Because the size of the crew was determined by the size of the sails, the challenge then became to reduce the size of the sails without losing total square footage (which translated into speed). Thus we see several innovations involving splitting the topsail horizontally into two sails.

As long ago as 1825 there was, on the American coast, a three-masted schooner called the *Pan Matanzas*, which had double topsails on her fore and main masts, and there were probably other ships similarly fitted in the coaster class which never had too many men. In 1844 and 1845, again in the United States, Captain R. B. Forbes fitted the double topsail into *Midas, Massachusetts* and *Edith*, auxiliary steamers with a big spread of canvas and far fewer men on deck than the ordinary sailing ship. Then, in the mid-'fifties, Captain Frederick Howes patented a similar idea with the particular view to having them fitted into Donald McKay's giant sailing ship, *Great Republic,* a ship of such size that ordinary single topsails would have required a man-of-war's watch to handle them. The advantages of the idea were soon appreciated; any number of ships already fitted with single topsails were changed to double, although some still retained the old single topsail on their mizzen mast, and all the new ships were given them in the first place. Later, the idea extended to the topgallants as well.

In the old single topsails the yard lowered down to the cap on lifts, but in modern double topsails the lower yard is fixed by a crane. There are no reef points in the lower topsail, it is the last sail to be taken in and the upper topsail fulfills the function of the reef; when it is furled the sail is equal to a close reefed topsail.

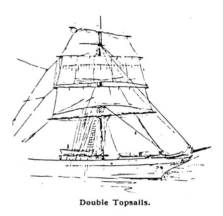

The upper topsail is sheeted to the yardarms of the lower topsail and its yard is lowered on a parrel when it is to be furled or reefed by halyards to the deck on opposite sides of the ship. In some old ships the upper topsails had two rows of reef points, but one was more general, and in many modern ships there are none at all.

Double Topsails.

Needless to say, the braces of the upper and lower topsail yards are independent to maintain a proper control. ['The Ship Modeller's Scrap Book," *Ships and Ship Models* 2, no. 13 (September 1932): 29-30]

And from Capt. Arthur Clark:

[The Forbes Rig] was eventually superseded by Howes's rig, which was invented by Captain Frederic Howes, of Brewster, Massachusetts, who in 1853 first put it on the ship *Climax*, of Boston, which he commanded. Captain Howes took out a United States Patent for his rig in 1854. In this rig, the lower topsail yard is slung by a truss at the lower mast cap; indeed, Howes's rig is the double topsail rig of the present day, though one does not often hear the name of Captain Howes in connection with it. [Arthur H. Clark, *The Clipper Ship Era (2nd ed., Riverside, CT, 1910), 236*]

And from a seaman who saw ships carrying the rig:

A big American ship occupied a berth ahead of us. It was fitted with double topsailyards, something new at that time. It was greatly ridiculed

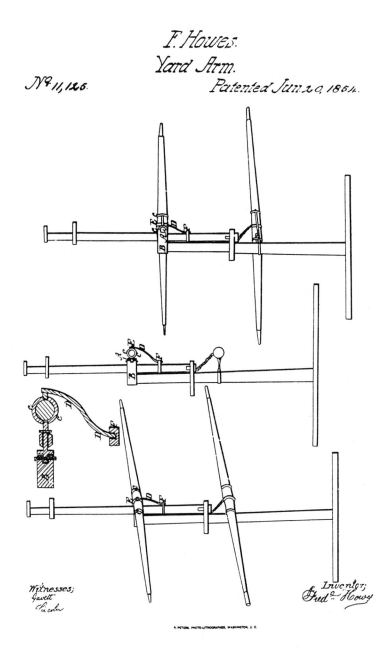

F. Howes.
Yard Arm.
Nº 11,126.
Patented Jun. 20, 1854.

Witnesses;
Gavett
Lincoln

Inventor;
Fredᵒ Howes

N. PETERS, PHOTO-LITHOGRAPHER, WASHINGTON, D.C.

Drawing of Howes' rig which accompanied his patent papers

UNITED STATES PATENT OFFICE.

FREDERIC HOWES, OF YARMOUTH, MASSACHUSETTS.

EXTRA YARD TO TOPSAILS.

Specification of Letters Patent No. 11,125, dated June 20, 1854.

To all whom it may concern:

Be it known that I, FREDERIC HOWES, of Yarmouth, in the county of Barnstable, the State of Massachusetts, have invented a new

5 and improved mode of applying and supporting a second or extra topsail-yard by means of a truss to the cap of the lower masthead, and also a crane or brace to the heel of the topmast, top, or trestletrees, to

10 the lower mast; and I do hereby declare that the following is a full and exact description thereof, reference being had to the accompanying drawings and to the letters of reference marked thereon.

15 The nature of my invention consists in applying an extra yard to any topsail, and supporting it upon the cap of the lower mast head by a truss and crane, as hereinafter described, so that the upper, topsail yard

20 may be lowered down in close proximity to the said extra yard. By this improvement the topsail is divided into two parts and may be reefed or taken in with one third the number of men necessary to secure the

25 same result in the old plan. When, as by the old plan, the yards are supported by a chain attached to the topmast above such yard the upper topsail yard cannot be lowered below the point of attachment of such

30 chain to the topmast, and of course the sail will be "bellied out" by the wind and require considerable tackle and a large number of men to take it in, but by my improvements the upper yard may be lowered

down to the new yard, and the upper half 35 of the topsail, as divided, drops behind the lower half of the sail, and after it is taken in or furled the lower half is clued in from the deck by the usual tackle and in the ordinary way. 40

The mode of applying and sustaining my new or extra yard is shown in elevation and in detail in the figures of the accompanying plate of drawings.

To enable others skilled in the art to make 45 and use my invention, I will proceed to describe its construction and operation.

I construct my yard in any of the known forms supported by a truss marked A in the accompanying drawing, attached to the 50 cap marked B, connected to the after part of the yard by iron bands c, c, on the forward part by a brace or crane, marked D, the upper end connected to the band marked E, by a swivel head, the lower end of the 55 brace or crane attached to the band marked F, by a pintle.

What I claim as my invention, and desire to secure by Letters Patent, is—

The application of an extra yard, sup- 60 ported by truss, crane, or brace, as herein described, or any other substantially the same, and which will produce the same effect.

FREDERIC HOWES.

Witnesses:
  E. E. RICE,
  NATHAN EDSON.

Specifications for Howes' rig as filed with the patent office

by the British, warning the world that they were working out then an invention on which they would patent. (Patent topsails). Well, they did! Even two. But both were fizzles. Men were hurt handling them in a gale and more than one ship was dismasted on account of it, whereas, that Yankee contraption double topsails was, within four years, generally adopted, first by the Germans, followed by the Scandinavians.
[Ferdinand Stolte, *Tales of the Sea . . . 1863 till 1869*]

APPENDIX B
OWNERS' ACCOUNTS

1. 1858, voyage 14 (May 1857-Oct 1858)

1858 Dec. 31

By balance a/c due owners carried to new a/c	6,082.24
Invoice of merchandise shipped on owners a/c	21,377.61

[signed] E. & O.C., Boston, Dec. 31st, 1858
          Howes & Crowell, per W. P. Ellison.

SHIP REVERE & OWNERS—in acct with Howes & Crowell

DR [Expenditures]

1857

May 8	To	Balance a/c due us	4,745.05
Aug 25	"	Cash paid carting	1.25
" 28	"	Prem. ins. on ship Bristol to Rio de Janeiro at and thence to Callao and Chinchas and thence to Valentia	
		12,000 @ 8-1/2% & pols $2 due Sept 11/58	1,022.00
		16,000 @ 9% & pols $2 do	1,442.00
Sep 11	"	Disbursements at Bristol and Newport	
		£1016.13.5 @ $4.80	4,880.02
Sep 18	"	Prem ins. on freight Newport to Rio de Janeiro	
		$5,000 @ 2% & pol. due Mar 7/58	101.00

1858

Mar 2	"	Disbs. of ship at Rio de Janeiro	2,242.56
Mar 15	"	Prem. ins. on freight Chinchas to Valencia	
		$20,000 @ 5% & pol. due Nov 4-5th/58	1,002.50

Mar 19	"	Commns. accepting and advancing funds to pay Capt. Rocko's draft fr. Callao a/c disbursements at that place $2,500 @ 2-1/2%	62.50
Apr 28	To	Disbursements at Callao	2,149.96
		do at Chinchas	668.87
Jun	"	Our comn negotiating draft on Royal Mail Steamship a/c freight to Rio de Janeiro £1,000 % 1%	48.00
Aug 6	"	Fire ins. one month in Valencia	50.00
Aug 20	"	Prem. ins. on ship at & from Valencia to Boston via Torrevieja $25,000 % 2-1/2%	603.00
Sep 20	"	Comn to Oakford & Co. on guano charter £134.4.8 10%	656.25
"	"	Bankers coms on money deposited with Baring Bros. & Co. £4,360.5.9 @ 1/2%	104.64
"	"	Coms negotiating drafts on Baring Bros. & Co. £4,360.5.9 @ 1%	209.29
Oct 8		Disbursements at Valencia	3,484.57
"		do Torrevieja	204.00
Oct 17	"	Entry fees, Custom House, Boston	53.67
"	"	Boatman, 75 cs. Wages to crew $1,396.33	1,397.80
"	"	Fire ins. in Harbor $10,000 1 mo.	25.00
Nov 9		Bill Ballast $55.44 Hauling $5	60.44
		Towing $54 inward Pilotage $26.29	80.29
"	"	Capt. wages Apr. 27/57 to Oct. 27/58 18 mos. @ $100 $1,800.00 less Hospital money 3.60	1,796.40
"	"	Scraping $3 Stevedore dischg $107.53	110.53
Dec 4	"	Bending sails $18 Sawing wood $18	36.00
Dec 9	"	Clearance $4.35 Adv. wages $548	552.35
		Board bill $11 Blocks $90	101.00
		Water $20 Sailmaking $146	166.00
		Outward pilotage $23.42 Bill Wood $69	92.42
"	"	Ship Keeper $72.14 Bill Beef &c. $169.37	241.31
"	"	Stevedore ldg $420 W. casks $83.60	503.60
"	"	H. C. Brooks & Co. bill Stores due Mar 26/59	668.38
"	"	H. Bird & Co., bill Pork &c., due Apr 3/59	641.00
Dec 9		Bill Hams $22 Rigger work $350	372.00
		Vinegar 2 bbls. $9.20 Shipwright $330	339.20
		Bill Duck $270 Preserved meats $43.46	313.46
		Repg caboose $36.57 Repg compass $4	40.57
		Repg steering apparatus $8.54 Flour $80	88.54
		Carpenter bill $73 Blacksmiths $206	279.00
		Sparmakers bill $300 Repg H. pump $9.50	309.50
		Bill Pigs, fouls & vegetables	80.00
		Beechers bill Carving head	51.50
		Ship chandlery $1,061.25 Paints &c. $227.75	1,289.00

Dec 9	H. A. Peirce coms & advertising ship for		
	Valparaiso	332.26	
	Repl. M Chest $11.75 Hawser pipes $23.90	40.65	
	Coopering $30.87 Postage $15	45.87	
Dec 31	Balance Interest due us	319.00	
	Comn on disbs. at Boston $9,474 @ 2-1/2%	236.85	
			34,340.53
	Balance a/c due owners carried to new a/c		6,082.24
			40,422.77

CR [Receipts]

1857			
Sep 11	By freight from St. John's to Bristol		
	£1,013.14.3 @ $4.80 [lumber]	4,865.82	
1858			
Mar 2	Freight from Bristol to Rio de Janeiro		
	£1,517.12 @ $4.80 [1.085T coal]	7,284.48	
Apr 28	Prem. on drafts recd. at Callao on us		
	a/c disbs. $2,500 @ 6%	150.20	
"	Sale launches at Callao	210.00	
	Prem. recd on draft on Royal Mail		
	Steamship Co. L1,000 @ 1-1/2%	66.66	
Oct 8	Charter Guano to Valencia 1,193T to Bent £4.10		
	£5,369.7.6 @ $4.80	25,770.00	
	Prem. recd on remittance £4,329.14.6	279.14	
Nov 15	Sales mats $3 Old junk $7.40	10.40	
Dec 31	Profits on cargo salt due May 28/59	1,783.27	
			40,422.77
	Amts. carried forward		40,422.77

2. 1859, voyage 15 (Dec 1858-Oct 1859)

SHIP REVERE'S ACCOUNT TO NOV. 19TH, 1859

SHIP REVERE & OWNERS — in acct with Howes & Crowell

DR [Expenditures]

1858

Dec 20	To	Prem. ins. on ship at and from Boston to Caldera via Valparaiso	
		$25,000 @ 2-1/2 & pol.	503.00
		Prem. ins. on freight as above $8,000	161.00

1859

Mar 19	Carting anchor on $1.50	
	Surveyor's certificate $15	16.50
Jun 29	2 coils cordage at Valparaiso	38.34
Jul 4	Prem. ins. on ship from Caldera to Balto [Baltimore] via ports to load	
	$25,000 @ 2-1/2% & pol.	628.00
"	Prem. ins. as above on freight $10,000	251.50
Jul 15	Disbursements at Valparaiso	1,994.25
Jul 29	" at Caldera	255.38
Sep 13	" at Cobra	104.00
"	Exchange on money remitted	221.91
Oct 10	Cash paid telegrams to & fr Balto	.90
Oct 17	do Fire ins. in Balto 1 mo. $20,000 @ 1/4%	50.00
Oct 20	Wages paid crew at Balto	1,412.75
"	Funds furnished by Capt. R.	269.20
"	Capts. wages from Oct. 27/58 to Oct. 11/59	
	11 ms. 16ds. @ $100	1153.33
	less Hospital money	2.00
		1,151.33
Nov 1	Cash paid mate a/c wages	30.00
	do S. D. Crane & Co., bal. comn due	
	Loring & Co. on copper ore charter	10.36
	Disbursements at Baltimore	3156.34
	Comn collecting charter copper ore	
	$10,414.41 @ 2-1/2%	260.36
Nov 19	Comn collecting drafts for Caldera	
	$4,015.80 @ 1%	40.16
		10,555.28
		23,913.73

Balance paid owners

I. Crowell 1/8 part is	1009.81
David K. Akin 1/16 " "	834.90
David Killey 1/16 " "	834.90
Silas Baker 1/32 " "	417.45

CR [Receipts]

1859

Jan 1	By balance a/c due ship	6,082.24
Feb 5	" Sale old anchor & chain	89.10
Mar 12	" deduction bill Salting pork	5.00
Jun 29	" One half amt profits cordage shipped to Valparaiso	161.89
Jul 15	Freight from Boston to Valparaiso	2,066.14
Sep 29	do to Caldera	4,015.80
"	Prm. recd on same	240.94
"	Freight from Valparaiso to Caldera	100.00
	Sale Boat at Caldera	100.00
Oct 31	Charter from Cobra to Balto	10,414.41
	Profits on rags shipped for dunnage [i.e., packing material]	271.21
Nov 19	Balance Interest due ship	367.00
		23,913.73
[signed]	E. & O. E., Boston, Nov. 19, 1859	
	Howes & Crowell per W. P. Ellison	23,913.73

3. 1862, voyage 17 (May 1861-Jul 1862)

SHIP *REVERE*'S ACCOUNT, 8 MO. 22^d 1862

DR [Expenditures]

1861

Feb 26	To	Prem. ins. on ship for one year from Nov. 5/60	
		$20,000 @ 7% pol.	1,404.00
Apr 30	"	Prem. ins. on freight from Boston to Valparaiso	
		via St. Johns $12,000 @ 3% & pol.	361.50
Jun 19	"	Cash paid Mate's wife	20.00
Jun 28		do telegram to New York	.40
Aug 5		do Carting contracted in May	2.90
Sep 12		do Mate's wife	20.00
Oct 4		do do	20.00
Nov 7		do do	20.00
"		Comn negotating draft on A. Gibbs Sr.	44.97
Nov 25		Prem. ins. on freight Coquimbo to Liverpool via	
		ports in South America	
		$10,000 @ 4% & pol.	401.00
		5,000 @ 5% & pol.	251.00
Dec 5		Cash paid owners	5,600.00
"		Comn on remittance from Valparaiso	
		Alsop & Co's draft	
		£810.14.7 @ 1%	39.00
"		Disbursements at Valparaiso	1,293.45
"	"	" Coquimbo	308.63
"		Remittances from Valparaiso	
		£ 945.12.6 costing	5,100.00
		£810.14.7 costing	4,300.00

1862

Feb 15	Prem. ins. on ship for one year from Nov. 5/61	
	$20,000 @ 7% & pols	1,404.00
Mar 10	Cash paid J. D. Brewste comn on charter guano	375.00
May 17	Disbursements at Cobija	215.60
"	do Callao	826.87
"	Comn on draft from Callao a/c disbursements at	
	that place 321.10 @ 1%	3.21
Jun 13	Disbursements at Liverpool	
	£ 620.9.10 @ 4.50	2,978.36
Jul 8	Entry fees Boston 44.68 Wages to crew 62.67	107.35
"	Shipkeeper 6 Pumping 4.50	10.50
Jul 17	Hauling 4 Dockage June 7.50	11.50
	Sundries furnished crew at sea	413.16
	Capts wages May 5/61 to July 18/62	
	14 ms 13 ds @ 125	1804.17
	less hospital	2.80 1801.37

		Inward pilotage 41.09 Towing 26	67.09	
Jul 29		Second Mate bal. wages & board	45.00	
		Bankers comn on deposit with Brown Shipley & Co.		
		£1300 @ 1/2%	55.20	
"		Comn negotiating drafts on the same 1%	110.40	
Jul 29		Addl prem. ins. on ship for carrying cargoes		
		guano & salt 1-1/2%	300.00	
"		brokerage on sale ship	225.00	
		B. Howes services delivery clerk	33.00	
		stevedore discharging salt &c.	191.12	
		sundry postage	16.00	
		comn on disbursements at Boston		
		$481.56 @ 2-1/2%	12.04	
				28,388.62
[Jul 29]		Balance forward owners		33,949.37
				62,337.99

CR [Receipts]

1861

Jul 15	By	Return comn on charter to Valparaiso being	
		expense of remitting	48.98
Nov 5		Cash recd draft on A. Gibbs Son London received	
		from Valparaiso £945.12.6 @ 7%	4,496.97
Dec 5		Freight from St. Johns to Valparaiso	
		& Coquimbo	11,109.45
		Addition as per Charter party	300.00
		Passage money // Mate's wife? //	50.00
		Cash recd draft on Alsop & Co. recd from	
		Valparaiso	
		£810.14.7 @ 8-1/4%	3,900.50

1862

May 17	Prem. recd on Chile money at Callao	
	370 @ 15%	55.50
	do on draft on us 321.10 @ 25%	80.27
May 20	Prem. ins. recd on draft on Brown Shipley & Co.	
	over $4.80 to a £	
	£1200 sold @ 13-5/8%	300.00
Jun 2	Prem. recd as above on 76.76 [sold] 14%	20.38
Jun 7	do 700 14-3/8%	198.33
Jun 13	do 300 16%	106.67
"	Charter guano to Liverpool	
	Nett amt £3,347.12.9 @ $4.80	16,068.66

Jul 29	Cash recd Baker & Morrill for 1/4 part of ship as per agreement	5,625.00	

	Baker & Morrill notes of equal amounts, with
	    interest, for four, six and nine months, for 3/4
	    part of ship as per agreement
		16,875.00	

Aug 7	Prem. ins. returned a/c policies cancelled	371.41	
	Nett profits salt [as per separate schedule]	2,370.87	
			62,337.99

Source: Manuscript in Yarmouth Port Historical Society; microfilm, courtesy of International Marine Archives, Nantucket, Massachusetts.

Appendix C
General Average

1. Definition

General average is a concept peculiar to maritime law. Basically, it provides that everyone involved in a voyage—shipowner and cargo owner alike—share the risks of the voyage in certain circumstances.

For general average to occur, three conditions must be met:

1. A common danger; a danger in which ship, cargo and crew all participate; a danger imminent and apparently 'inevitable,' except by voluntarily incurring the loss of a portion of the whole to save the remainder.

2. There must be a voluntary jettison, or casting away, of some portion of the joint concern for the purpose of avoiding this imminent peril or, in other words, a transfer of the peril from the whole to a particular portion of the whole.

3. This attempt to avoid the imminent common peril must be successful.

The following example, although simplified, demonstrates how general average is calculated:

A vessel is under charter and worth $1,000,000 and carries cargo belonging to one owner worth $1,000,000. The freight to be earned on arrival is worth $100,000. In a storm it becomes necessary to throw overboard, in order to save the ship, cargo worth $100,000, freight on which, if it had arrived, would have been $10,000, and, in order to accomplish the jettison in a hurry, it becomes necessary to cut a hole in the deck over the hold, damaging the ship to the extent of $5,000. The "vessel interest" (ship plus freight) was worth, as a whole, $1,100,000, and has incurred a total damage of $15,000 (injury to deck plus loss of freight). The cargo was worth $1,000,000, and has been damaged $100,000 worth. All three interests together were worth $2,100,000, and were damaged by the general average acts in the total amount of $115,000, or 115 parts in 2100. The end to be reached by calculation is that each interest shall suffer in just this proportion. The application of this proportion to the cargo interest at risk ($1,000,000) gives, to the nearest cent, $54,761.90; and the same proportion of the vessel interest (ship and freight) totalling $1,100,000 comes to $60,238.10. Since the cargo, by jettison, has suffered $100,000, a sum greater than its proper share of the loss, the ship must pay to the cargo owner the difference between that amount and the $54,761.90 the cargo should end up out of pocket, or $45,238.10. This payment, together with the $15,000 it has suffered by lost freight and damage to the deck, will put the ship out of pocket to a total of $60,238.10, which is its proper proportion of the general average loss.

Source: Grant Gilmore and Charles L. Black, Jr., *The Law of Admiralty*, 220-24.

2. DISBURSEMENTS IN CONSEQUENCE OF DISASTER, DECEMBER 1880

Disbursements		General average	Owners
Laborers on vessel (8, including 2 Indians)	54.50	5.50	
Wm. Farrell: boathire 9 trips to & from vessel with master	5.50	5.50	
Moodyville Saw Mills Co., "for lumber; drayage to Esquimalt."	7.70	7.70	
Drake & Jackson, notaries	7.50	7.50	
J. G. Howard "for carriage hire conveying master to and from Victoria	4.50	4.50	
S. H. Wilton "for repairing fore sail injured at sea"	21.20		21.20
U.S. Consulate "for tonnage fees"	8.25	8.25	
Welch, Rithet & Co., "for telegrams paid to San Francisco relative to instructions"	6.20	6.20	
Stevedore, "for discharging coal 838-24/42 tons coal at Esquimalt @ 50%"	419.32	419.32	
S. McQuade & son, for axe, 25 ft. rubber hose, lantern, 1 bolt duck, gauge glass, 1	73.32		73.32
coil 2-1/2 manila, 1 coil 3-1/2 manila	93.32	36.60	
"for falls in discharging," 30 fathoms			
4 in. manila "for engine while dis-	16.92	16.92	
charging," 2 lbs. boatnails, 1 wrench,	1.51		1.51
10 yds. duck, 15 lbs. rope, 5 yds.	8.70		8.70
duck & yarn			
Steam tug, "for towage from			105.03
Esquimalt to Victoria, from			
Victoria to sea"	55.00	55.00	

Cargo and Freight Jettisoned

The following coal was jettisoned or lost during forced discharge.

		General average	Owners
Original cargo		1165 tons	
less			
Delivered at Esquimalt and Victoria	838-27/42		
Delivered at San Francisco	217-1140/2240		
	1056-240/2240		
Difference	108-1900/2240		
@ $7.75 per ton		843.58	
less freight	435.39		
& duty	81.64		
		517.03	
		326.55	326.55

Disbursements	Items	General average	Owners

Freight
    Upon the foregoing 108-1900/2240 tons
        lost through jettison and forced discharge

@ $4 pr. ton	435.39	435.39	

Chas. Murray, "for passage to and from
    Victoria and services on board the

vessel."	160.00	160.00	

Mr. Kentfield "for telegrams sent to Victoria
    giving instructions as to the course to be

taken relative to cargo, &c."	48.05	48.05	

Wages and Provisions / Vessel's Company

Wages "from date of changing his course to seek a port of relief and repairs
    Decr. 8th until the cargo was discharged at Victoria January 1st 24/31"

Master	@125 per month	
1st mate	55 " "	
2nd do	40 " "	
cook	60 " "	
8 seamen @ $35 ea	280 " "	
	560.00	

	Items	General average
for 24/31 of a month	433.55	433.55

Provisions for same period		
Master	1.50 per day	
2 mates	1.50 " "	
9 men @ .40	3.60 " "	
	6.60 per day for 24 days	

	Items	General average
	158.40	158.40

Merchants' commission "for paying
    disbursements at Victoria and

	Items	General average
San Francisco" $934.46 @ 5%	46.72	46.72

C.V.S. Gibbs "for professional services
    and for this adjustment of general

	Items	General average
average"	100.00	100.00

Merchants' Commission "for collecting and

	Items	General average
settling General Average" $2330.35 @ 5%	116.52	116.52

	General average	Owners
GENERAL AVERAGE	2,446.87	
OWNERS		104.72

Contributory Interest and Apportionment

Vessel	Items	Contributory Values	General Average
Valued in the condition in which she arrived at this port	8,000.00		1,583.04
Freights: upon 217-1140/2240 tons delivered at San Francisco	870.04		
One half	435.02		
ADD			
Made good	453.39		
	870.41	870.41	172.24

Cargo

838-27/42 tons delivered at Victoria &c. @ $3	2,515.93		
217-1140/2240 tons delivered at San Francisco @ $7.75	1,685.69		
		4,201.62	
less: Freight 870.04			
Duty 163.13		1,033.17	
		3,168.45	
Add			
Contributed for loss through jettison and discharge	326.55	3,495.00	691.59
		12,365.41	2,446.87

The following disbursements were incurred after a portion of cargo was discharged at British Columbia, the same having left the vessel not again to be returned, all charges upon said coal ceases and the vessel, with freight and cargo remaining on board contributed to the following general average expenses.

Disbursements	Items	General Average	Owners
Port Blakely Mill Co.: telegrams, copper tacks, work, pitch, oakum, turpentine, copper nails, caulking all — "for temporary repairs to enable vessel to reach this port, charge same to general average": itemized items: telegrams, duck, welding, repairing truck, towage to Utsalady for discharge.		136.75	8.10
For wharfage on coal discharged, and water	197.35	50.00	2.50
Stevedores, bill for discharging coal to repair, and 250 tons @ 50%	250.00	250.00	
Steam tug "Mastick" towage, Victoria to Port Blakely	100.00	100.00	

	Items	General Average	Owners
Wages and Provisions of Vessel's Company			
Wages for 15/31 month "from date of leaving Victoria until the coal was reloaded Jany. 16th "	270.97	270.97	
Provisions: Master 1.50			
2 mates @ .75 1.50			
9 men @ .40 3.60			
$6.60 per day for 15 days	99.00	99.00	
Merchants commissions for paying bills $536.75 @ 5%		26.83	
C.V.S. Gibbs for this adjustment		50.00	
Merchants commissions for collecting general average $993.55 @ 5%		49.68	
GENERAL AVERAGE		1,033.23	
OWNERS			10.60
Contributory Interest and Apportionment			
Vessel valued at 8,000.00			
less: Propn of General Average 1,583.04			
6,416.96		6,416.96	909.71
Freight			
upon delivery at San			
Francisco 870.04			
less one half 435.02			
less Propn. of General			
Average 86.08			
348.94		348.94	49.46
Cargo			
upon 217-1140/ tons delivered at San Francisco			
less			
duty 163.13			
freight 870.04 1,033.17			
652.52			
less			
Propn. of General Average 130.12			
522.40	522.40	74.06	
		7,288.30	1,033.23

Settlement

OWNERS OF CARGO	Dr	Cr	To pay	Receive
Propn of 1st General Average	691.59			
Propn of 2nd " "	74.06			
Allowance for jettison and damage		326.55		
Balance to pay		439.10	439.10	
			less 100	
			dollars	
[endorsed]: $439.10				
	765.65	765.65		

OWNERS OF VESSEL

	Dr	Cr	To pay	Receive
Propn of 1st General Average	1,583.04			
Propn of 2nd " "	909.71			
Propn on Freight	172.24			
"	49.46			
Charges to Owners, 1st Average	104.72			
" 2nd Average	10.60			
Allowance for Freight jettisoned		435.39		
" Wages: 1st Average		433.55		
" Provisions "		158.40		
" Wages: 2nd "		270.97		
" Provisions "		99.00		
		1,432.46	1,432.46	
Balance to Pay	2,829.77	2,829.77		
Carried forward			1,871.56	

Agents of Vessel (for bills paid & to be paid):			
Disbursements at Victoria	671.41		
Steam tug	55.00		
Chas. Murray	160.00		
John Kentfield	48.05	}	1st average
Merchants' Commissions	46.72		
C.V.S Gibbs	100.00		
Merchants' Commissions	116.52		
Port Blakely Mill Co.	197.35		
Stevedores' bill	250.00		
Steam tug "Mastick"	100.00	}	2nd average
Merchants' Commissions	26.83		
C.V.S. Gibbs	50.00		
Merchants' Commissions	49.68		
	1,871.56		1,871.56
[signed] C. V. S. Gibbs, adjuster		1,871.56	1,871.56

Source: Kentfield Papers 90/7. See also chapter 4 of text, for the statement of C. Thos. Hopkins regarding the settlement.

ABBREVIATIONS

BC	*Boston Cultivator*
BDA	*Boston Daily Advertiser*
BET	*Boston Evening Transcript*
BPL	Boston Public Library
BSL	*Boston Shipping List and Prices Current*
DAB	*Dictionary of American Biography*
DAC	*Daily Alta California*
FARC	Federal Archives and Records Collection, Waltham, MA
FH log	Frederic Howes' journal
KP	Kentfield Papers
NA, RG	National Archives, Record Group [number supplied]
NYJC	*New York Journal of Commerce*
OED	*Oxford English Dictionary*
S&CL	*New York Shipping and Commercial List*
WA	*Puget Sound Weekly Argus*

NOTES

Chapter 1

[1] Morison, 225-26.

[2] Grace Lee Nute, "American Foreign Commerce (1825-1850)" (Ph.D. diss., Radcliffe College, 1921), 424.

[3] *See* Hall Gleason, 72; Carl Seaburg and Alan Seaburg, *Medford on the Mystic* (Medford, 1980), 81-89.

[4] The *Revere*'s documentation records may be found under her official number, #21620, at GSA, Industrial and Social Branch, National Archives and Records Service, Washington, D.C. 20408.

[5] Howes, *Autobiographical Sketch.*

[6] Simeon L. Deyo, ed., *History of Barnstable County, Massachusetts* (New York, 1890); Joshua Crowell Howes, *Genealogy of the Howes Family in America. Descendants of Thomas Howes, Yarmouth, Mass., 1637-1892* (Yarmouthport, 1892); Henry C. Kittredge, *Shipmasters of Cape Cod* (Boston and New York, 1935); U.S. Census, Massachusetts 1850, s.v. "Yarmouth."

[7] BSL, 3 Nov, 12 Dec 1849; 19 Jan, 6 Feb 1850; BET, 11 Dec 1849, 17 Jan 1850; *New Orleans Daily Picayune*, 17 Jan 1850; FH log; U.S. Hydrographic Office, *Navigation of the Caribbean Sea.*

[8] *See* appendix C; OED, s.v. "average, general"; *Encyl. Brit.*, 15th ed., Micropædia, s.v. "Average," "Maritime law."

[9] NA, RG 92, box 88, 10/27/f, "Revere."

[10] NA, RG 36 New Orleans, inward coastwise manifest, 16 Jan 1850.

[11] S & CL, 24 and 29 Apr, 27 Jul 1850; BET, 21 May, 25 Jul; FH log; BSL, 17 jul; NA, RG 36 New York, returned crew list; NYJC, 6 Apr 1850.

[12] NA, RG 59 Liverpool, roll #10, "Return of arrivals and departures of American vessels, Quarter ending 30 June 1850"; Bradford, *Mariner's Dictionary*, 53

[13] Morison, 235.

[14] *London Evening Sun*, 29 and 31 May, and *Manchester Guardian*, 3 and 6 Jul 1850; S&CL, 31 Jul 1850. *See also* Francis H. Gleason, 795-97.

[15] S&CL, 15 Aug, 5 Oct 1850; BDA, 20 Aug; BSL, 30 Oct, 16 Nov, 18 Dec; *London Evening Sun,* 11 Nov; NA, RG 36 New York, articles of engagement, 14 Aug 1850; FH log.

[16] NA, RG 36, Boston passenger lists, roll #36, item #1021.

[17] BSL, 21 Dec 1850; District Court Records, March term 1851, pp. 343-44, and docket #64 (FARC).

[18] BSL, 25 Dec 1850; 22 Feb, 5 and 19 and 26 Mar 1851; BDA, 9 and 15 Jan, 24-26 Mar 1851; FH log.

[19] NA, RG 59 Liverpool, roll #1; RG 85 Liverpool, C28, vol. 7, p. 768; BDA, 10 Jan 1851.

[20] Morison, 231-32; DAB, *s.v.* "Train, Enoch." For an excellent treatment of packets, their design, function, specifications, amenities [or lack thereof], and history, *see* William A. Baker, *A Maritime History of Bath, Maine, and the Kennebec River Region* (2 vols., Bath, Maine, 1973), 1: 333-38 and 384-401.

[21] Pratt, David H., and Paul F. Smart, "Life on Board a Mormon Emigrant Ship," in *World Conference on Records Preserving Our Heritage*, August 12-15, 1980, vol. 5: British Family and Local History, part 1, series no. 418.

[22] NA, RG 36, Boston passenger lists, roll #37, item #295; BSL, 26 Mar 1851; BET, 24 Mar 1651.

[23] BDA, 10 and 15 Apr, 29 May; *St. John Morning News*, 15 Apr; NA, RG 59 St. John, roll #2; ibid. Liverpool, roll #11; NA, RG 36 New York, returned crew list, 5 Aug 1851; FH log. For interim reports, *see* BDA, 4 and 15 Aug 1851; BSL, 25 Jun, 9 and 13 Aug; S&CL, 9 Aug.

[24] S&CL, 30 Aug, 13 Sep, 31 Dec 1851; BSL, 24 Sep, 29 Oct, 1 Nov; NA, RG 36 New York, returned crew list, 27 Dec 1851; FH log; *St. John Morning News*, 13 and 19 Sep.

[25] NA, RG 59 St. John, roll #2; ibid. Liverpool, roll #11; RG 84 Liverpool, C28, vol. 6, p. 511, and C7.2, vol. 5, p. 11.

[26] Julian Hawthorne, *Hawthorne and His Circle* (New York, 1903), 183.

[27] S&CL, 31 Jan 1852; BET, 24 Feb; *New Orleans Daily Picayune*, 10 Feb; BSL, 31 Mar, 10 Apr; FH log; NA, RG 36 Mobile, tonnage abstract, 18 Mar 1852; BSL, 14 Apr 1852. The designated consignees were Read, Chadwick & Dexter, H. Bartlett, E. C. Bates, B. Wheatland,

T. G. Cary, J. P. Putnam, E. Baldwin, G. W. Abbott, and 50 bales to "order."

[28] BSL, 21 Apr, 31 Jul, 18 Aug 1852; FH log; *Navigation*, as in n.7, above.

[29] *Mobile Daily Register*, 28 May 1852.

[30] Lyon, *Clipper Ships and Captains*, 70, 72.

[31] BSL, 4 Aug 1852; NA, RG 59, Turks Island, roll #4; RG 36, Mobile, captain's bond for seamen, cancelled Aug 1852 at Boston.

[32] *Extracts from the Evidence in Several Infringement Suits and in the Application for Extension of Patent, Brought and Made by Frederick Howes of Boston,* etc. (Boston, 1869), 32.

[33] Biographical note on Osborn Howes by his son Osborn Howes, Jr., in *Professional and Industrial History of Suffolk County, Massachusetts* (Boston, 1894), 2: 547n.

[34] Patent Office, #11,125, documents, 15 Feb 1853 to 20 Jun 1854, include a supporting letter from Howes & Crowell, 10 May 1853; BDA, 23 Jul, 25 Aug, 13 Nov 1855. Captain Howes licensed use of the rig, which "could be installed easily without major changes on any vessel," for a fee of eight cents per ton measurement. An undated manuscript list of 1,616 vessels with the rig installed shows that 1,078 "have paid fees either in full or in part"; the remaining 538—the *Revere* among them— "have not paid any thing" (NA, RG 241, Extension files).

Chapter 2

[1] Morison, 367.

[2] BC, 17 Sep 1852, p. 136. The BC published Swett's reports of the progress of the ship as received [not necessarily in the order written], and later his commentaries on life in the Feather River region, San Francisco and San Jose (1853-1856), which are currently being edited for eventual publication, along with a few letters to the *American Union* [also of Boston].

[3] Cluff, "John Swett's Diary," 291-92; Swett, *Public Education in California,* passim.

[4] BC, 23 Apr 1853, 136.

[5] Lyon, 62, 99.

[6] BC, 16 Jul 1853, p. 232; continued, 23 Jul 1853, p. 240.

[7] BC, 30 Jul 1853, p. 248; continued, 6 Aug 1853, p. 256.

[8] BC, 9 Apr 1853, p. 120.

[9] Ibid.; Cluff, 291; DAC, 1 Feb 1853. In the BC issue for 5 March 1853, Otis Brewer, editor and owner, announced "the safe arrival of our universal friend and favorite Jack, in the land of gold, as also the receipt of a packet of letters."

[10] Letter from San Francisco, 15 Dec 1853, in BC, 11 Feb 1854, p. 50; Hittell, *History*, 215-17.

[11] Letter from San Francisco, 1 and 5 Feb 1853, in BC, 16 Apr 1853, p. 128, and 26 Mar 1853, p. 102.

[12] For Morrill, see *War of the Rebellion, Official Records* (Washington, D.C.), ser. 1, v. 48, pt. 2, p. 275, and v. 50, pt. 1, p. 735. For Swett: Roy M. Cloud, *Education in California: Leaders, Organizations and Accomplishments of the First Hundred Years* (Stanford, California, 1952), 53. I am indebted to Mr. Kenneth C. Cramer, archivist of the Dartmouth College Library, for providing copies of a necrology of Mr. Swett and a "Summary of Educational Positions Held and Bibliography of Educational Papers," annotated by Mrs. Swett. For both men, *see* San Francisco city directories.

[13] For place-names, cf. Horsburgh, *India Directory*.

[14] NA, RG 59 Manila, roll #1.

[15] NA, RG 59 St. Helena, roll #9.

[16] "Sea-time," as cited in logs, was a concept peculiar to navigators, who computed the position of the ship for noon. They determined latitude by observations of the sun, and longitude generally also in the daytime. The navigator's day that began at noon on 11 March was mid-day of 10 March civil time. At midnight civil time caught up to sea-time, and they shared the date until the following noon, when 12 March began for the navigator. Thus the stated day of the week was likewise a half-day ahead of the civil day, with Wednesday p.m. sea-time being Tuesday p.m. civil time, and listed the following morning in the logs as "Wednesday a.m." and hence in agreement with civil time. [*Encyclopedia Britannica*, 11th ed., *s.v.* "Time, measurement of" and "Time, standard."] In citing the logs of captains Howes and Hamilton, I have converted the entries into civil time.

Chapter 3

[1] NA, RG 41 Boston, perm. reg. #441; RG 41, Boston, bills of sale of registered vessels, vol. 6, pp. 269, 270. For news of the voyage, *see* reports in BSL, 12 Nov 1853; ibid., 12 Apr, 13 May, 24 and 28 Jun 1854;

BDA, 14 Nov 1853; BDA, 18 Mar and 11 May 1854; BET, 1 May 1854; S&CL, 13 May 1854.

[2] Whidden, 102-7, *passim*.

[3] NA, RG 84, Port Stanley, C22, "Marine Notes of Protest."

[4] NA, RG 59, Port Stanley, roll #7; Whidden, 107, 110.

[5] BSL, 1, 5, 8 Jul, 13 Dec 1854; ibid., 17 Jan, 11 Apr, 13 Jun, 8 and 29 Aug 1855.

[6] NA, RG 84 Liverpool, C28, v. 13, p. 88; ibid., C22, v. 12; ibid., C7.2, v. 6, p. 87; RG 59 Liverpool, roll #13.

[7] NA, RG 59 Callao, roll #1, return of arrivals and departures of American vessels, 1 Jul 1854-30 Jun 1855; ibid., Consul Wm. Miles to Wm. Marcy, Sec'y of State, 25 Nov 1854; *Hunt's* 34 (1856), 450.

[8] Rutter, "South American Trade of Baltimore," 36-49, 76-78; *Hunt's*, 34 (1856), 430-31; 35 (1856), 106-7; 36 (1857), 638.

[9] BSL, 20 and 29 Aug 1855; NYSL, 29 Aug 1855.

[10] FARC, Sep. term 1855, v. 38, p. 600, and docket #59.

[11] I am indebted to Mr. William F. King, Jr., of Woolwich, Maine, for this note from the firm's ledger.

[12] BDA, 19, 20 Sep 1855. For news en route, *see* BSL, 8, 15, 22 Sep 1855; DAC, 16 Oct; BSL, 9 Jan, 19 Mar, 16 Apr, 14 May, 11 Jun, 9 Jul 1856.

[13] NA, RG 59 Callao, roll #2; Winsor, *Memorial History* 4: 222; Morison, 366; BSL, 19 Sep 1855.

[14] Morison, 280-83, 366; Alistair Cooke, *America* (1973), 372-73; DAB, *s.v.* "Tudor, Frederic."

[15] NA, RG 84 Callao, C1.1, "Record of Treasury fees, 1853-1859."

[16] NA, RG 36 Philadelphia, inward foreign cargo manifest and surrendered crew list, 1 Jul 1856.

[17] NA, RG 36 Philadelphia, outward foreign cargo manifest, 19 Aug 1856. For news of the voyage, *see* BSL, 23 and 27 Aug, 10 Sep, 8 and 22 Oct, 9 and 19 Nov, 1856; ibid., 11 Feb; 2, 11, and 25 Mar; 8, 15, 18 Apr 1857.

[18] BSL, 3 and 13 Dec 1856.

[19] NA, RG 59 London, roll #25; ibid., Elsinore, roll #3; NA, RG 84 Elsinore, C37, "Record of the arrival and departure of American vessels." For the law of general average, *see* appendix C.

[20] BSL, 2 and 6 May 1857.

[21] NA, RG 59 St. John, roll #2; ibid., RG 59 Bristol, roll #5; *St. John Morning News*, 11 and 25 May 1857. For news of the voyage, *see* BSL,

3 and 17 Jun, 15 Jul, 26 Aug 1857; ibid., 17 Feb, 17 Mar, 14 Apr, 12 May, 1 Sep, 23 Oct 1858.

[22] NA, RG 84 Rio de Janeiro, C20, vol. 270, "Crew lists, 1855-1859"; ibid., Callao, C1.1, "Record of fees," vol. 3, and C24.4: "Ship's Daily Journal"; NA, RG 59 Callao, roll #3: Miles to Marcy; NA, RG 59 Valencia, roll #2.

[23] For news of the voyage, see BSL, 11 and 22 Dec 1858; ibid., 20 Apr, 11 May, 1 and 22 Jun, 13 Jul, 24 Aug; 1, 15, 22, and 26 Oct 1859.

[24] NA, RG 36 Baltimore, crew list issued at Boston, 9 Dec 1858, surrendered at Baltimore, 10 Oct 1859.

[25] NA, RG 59 Valparaiso, roll #6.

[26] NA, RG 36 Baltimore, register of vessels showing cargo from Cobra; Rutter, 38 [402].

[27] NA, RG 59 Antwerp, roll #5; Howes, 149.

[28] *Mobile Daily Register*, 28 Nov 1859; BSL, 9 Nov and 7 Dec 1859; NA, RG 36 Mobile, inward coastwise cargo manifest, 30 Nov 1859, and outward foreign cargo manifest, 28 Dec 1859; NA, RG 59 Havre, roll #9. For later news of voyage, see BSL, 11, 14, 18 Jan, 29 Feb, 21 Mar, 11 Apr, 11 Jul, 14 Nov, 5 and 26 Dec 1860; ibid., 6 and 27 Feb, 13 and 27 Mar 1861; *North China Herald*, 11 Aug, 6 Oct, 3 and 17 Nov 1860.

[29] Morison, 299; NA, RG 84 Shanghai, C20, v. 1, "Arrival and departure of American vessels, 1858-1874."

[30] NA, RG 84 Shanghai, C23, "Marine Extended Protest," vol. 1.

[31] NA, RG 59 Shanghai, roll #5, "Quarterly return and statement of fees received"; NA, RG 84 Canton, C20; NA, RG 59 Manila, roll #2.

[32] BSL, 10 and 27 Apr, 8 May 1861.

[33] NA, RG 59 St. John, N.B., roll #2; ibid., Valparaiso, roll #6; ibid., Cobija, roll #1. For further news of the voyage, see BSL, 11 May, 11 Jun, 25 Sep, 6 and 20 Nov, 4 and 18 Dec 1861; ibid., 14 May, 14 Jun, 9, 16, 23 Jul; 2, 6, 9, 16 Aug 1862; S&CL, 18 Jun 1862; Yarmouth Port Hist. Soc., Doc. 1.49, "*Revere*/ship," account dated 22 Aug 1862 (appendix B.3).

[34] NA, RG 59 Callao, M155, roll #4, "return of arrival and departure of American vessels" and "return of consular fees," 1 Jan 1858-30 Jun 1858; NA, RG 84 Liverpool, C20: vol. 1, "Arrivals and departures of American vessels"; ibid., C22, vol. 25.

[35] Morison, 368, 365; Gleason, *Old Ships*, 72-78; *Professional and Industrial History of Suffolk County, Massachusetts*, 2: 548.

[36] NA, RG 41 Boston, bills of sale for registered vessels, vol. 25, pp. 63, 118. Oliver Eldridge was a native of Yarmouth, Cape Cod, who went

to sea at an early age, was promoted to captain in 1840, and commanded vessels belonging to the Dramatic Line, between New York and Liverpool. During the Civil War he was captain of the "splendid steamer *Atlantic*," the flagship of General Sherman, commanding the expeditionary corps at Fort Royal. Prior to 1864 Eldridge had brought the steamer *Constitution* to San Francisco, and in that year he arrived with his family from New York on the *Golden City* to take up permanent residence. He became local agent for the Pacific Mail Steamship Company, and later for the New York Board of Underwriters, and was also a director of the Pacific Telephone Company and of other corporations (Zoeth Eldredge, ed., *History of California*, 5 vols., New York, 1915), 4: 384; San Francisco city directories). Eldridge held his *Revere* shares until the vessel was sold to the Kentfield interest in 1865.

[37] MS., Massachusetts vol. 71, p. 200Y, R. G. Dun & Co., Collection, Baker Library, Harvard University Graduate School of Business Administration; BPL, Boston City Documents: "List of persons, copartnerships & corporations, who were taxed . . . " [microfilm], 1862, and Assessors' "Street" books (MS.), 1862, ward 4.

[38] NA, RG 41 Boston, permanent register #199; NA, RG 36 New York, temporary reg. #486, 23 Nov 1863. For news of the voyage, *see* BSL, 23 Aug, 12 Nov, 10 Dec 1862; ibid., 21 Jan, 15 Apr, 13 and 30 May, 10 and 24 Jun 1863.

[39] *Hunt's* 34 (1856), 435-41.

[40] NA, RG 59 Singapore, roll #2; NA, RG 84 Singapore, C24, v. 2; ibid., C 1.1, "record of quarterly statement of fees."

[41] S&CL, 9 Sep 1863; Boston city directory.

[42] NA, RG 41 New York, bills of sale for registered vessels, vol. 43, p. 148.

[43] NA, RG 36 New York, temporary reg. #486, 23 Nov 1863; NA, RG 41 San Francisco, returned crew list, 29 Apr 1864; Lloyd's *Register* 1864. For news of the voyage, *see also* S&CL, 28 and 31 Oct, 7 and 25 Nov 1863; ibid., 4 May 1864; BSL, 9 Dec 1863 and 4 May 1864; DAC, 29 Apr 1864.

[44] NA, RG 41 San Francisco, "temporary" reg. #69, 20 May 1864.

[45] Ibid., "temporary" reg. #87, 17 Apr 1865; ibid., permanent enrollment #173, 21 Nov 1865. For news of the voyage, *see* S&CL, 29 Jun 1864, 15 Feb 1865; BSL, 6 Jul, 3 and 31 Aug 1864; ibid., 1 and 25 Jan, 8 Feb, 4 and 18 Mar, 6, 19, and 20 Apr, 3 May 1865; DAC, 24 May 1864, 23 Mar 1865; NA, RG 36 San Francisco, returned crew list, 22 Mar 1865.

[46] DAC, 18 Apr, 18 Jun 1865; BSL, 17 May, 28 Jun, 29 Jul 1865; NA, RG 36 San Francisco, returned crew list, 17 Jun 1865.

Chapter 4

[1] NA, RG 41 San Francisco, bills of sale of registered vessels, 12 Sep 1865.

[2] Weidberg, "History of John Kentfield and Company"; Hittell, *Commerce*, 594.

[3] I am indebted to the California State Library and to Mrs. M. K. Swingle, reference librarian of the California Historical Society, for information about the share-owners.

[4] Vital Records, Hardwick, MA; *San Francisco Call*, 20 Mar 1909, p. 11, c.4; San Francisco city directories.

GENERAL NOTE: For the subsequent history of the Revere and her voyages, the Kentfield Papers and the Daily Alta California are the chief sources. Since the manuscripts are for the most part in chronological sequence, and since the local maritime news was usually printed within twenty-four hours of the event, citations of sources for individual voyages seem superfluous. For quoted texts, events of special interest, delayed reports, and clarification, however, documentation is provided in the notes.

[5] For figures on commerce, population and immigration, *see* Hittell, *History*, 196-99, 215, 491-94, and *Resources* (any edition); Soulé, *Annals,* 495-96; *Hunt's*, 56 (1857): 140-41, 146-47, and (1864): 419. For further information on some of the mills and their owners, *see* Hittell, *Commerce*, 196-206 and 590ff.

[6] NA, RG 36 San Francisco, returned crew list, 21 Aug 1865.

[7] Ibid., 15 Nov 1865.

[8] Following the permanent enrollment issued at San Francisco on 21 Nov 1865, and prior to the permanent register issued on 22 Jan 1878, there was a series of enrollments and registers, permanent and temporary, as the ship's destination changed between the Washington Territory and the Hawaiian Islands. The intervening documents were:

> #128 p.r., 18 Apr 1866
> #155E, 9 Mar 1871
> #63 p.r., 10 Apr 1872
> #37E, 7 Aug 1872

#6 t.r., 22 Aug 1873 (Pt Townsend)

#127 p.e., 8 Dec 1873

#45 p.e., 5 Aug 1875

#22 p.r., 4 Nov 1875

[9] Permanent register #128, 18 Apr 1866 (NA, RG 36 San Francisco). McIntyre was born in Scotland in 1831 (ibid., returned crew list, 19 Jun 1865) and arrived in Victoria in 1854 on the *Marquis of Bute*. From there he went to San Francisco and, in 1859, took command of the bark *Ann Parry*, owned by Capt. George Chase (*Lewis & Dryden*, 165 n.15).

[10] Buchanan, 48; KP 91/9; DAC, 15-22 Mar 1873.

[11] First mate was Thomas J. Conner, born in New York (shipping articles, 3-14 Jul 1873, in KP 91/9); DAC, 15-22 Mar 1873.

[12] WA, 18 Jul and 1 Aug 1874.

[13] Buchanan, 48.

[14] Shipping articles, 10 Jun 1875 (KP 91/4); WA, 10 Jul 1875; permanent enrollment #45, 5 Aug 1875, because "rig changed from ship to bark" (NA, RG 41 San Francisco). Bills in KP, including charges for hotel and board of crew, with 184 meals @ 20¢.

[15] Assessment figures in KP 91/2, 91/6, 91/9, 92/3, 92/8, 93/2.

[16] Bill from Lorenzo Foard, 5 Stewart St., for 1,775M ft. hemp rope @ .04-1/2; 75M ft. manila rope @ .01-1/4 (KP ?/4); from John L. Prior, sailmaker, 304 Davis St., $346.64, for a mainsail (431 yds, no. 3 @ 52¢ per yd.), lower main & topsail (217 yds. no.1 @ 56¢ per yd.), and cartage ($1.00). Tonnage duties for the year 1876, based on the re-measurement figures of 829.33T, were charged to Berryman & Doyle (NA, San Bruno, RA 14). Also based on the re-measurement were the charges of the pilot, W. H. Jolliffe: $66.58, @ $2.50 per drawing 20 ft., plus 2¢ per ton ($50.00 + 16.58).

[17] Buchanan, 49-50; tonnage duties paid by Rosenfeld, 29 Dec 1876 (NA, San Bruno, "Record of tonnage duties"); shipping articles, 31 Dec 1875, "for Departure Bay or any other port in Vancouver Island or Puget Sound"; also, returned crew list (NA, RG 36 San Francisco); WA, 21 Jan 1876; consignor also liable for tonnage duties at San Francisco (NA, San Bruno, MS. "Record of tonnage duties").

[18] Shipping articles, 25 Feb—6 Mar, 1876; WA, 14 Apr 1876.

[19] Of the five payments, unitemized, made to Calvin Paige between 8 March and 7 July, $432.78 and 366.45 may have been returns on his shares, but the larger, round amounts of $4,000, $8,450, and $9,450 seem hardly to fit the category (KP 91/6, 9).

[20] KP 93/1: bills from DAC and Guide Publishing Co.

[21] Carpenter's bill, $508.75 (KP 93/1).

[22] WA, 6 Feb 1879.

[23] Welch, Rithet & Co. had established themselves in Victoria in 1871 as "commission merchants, and shipping and insurance agents" (Hittell, *Commerce*, 206). Copies of telegrams in KP 93/1.

[24] On 26 July at Victoria, McIntyre paid $15 for "service and boat hire off [*illegible*] Island ended owing to intercept ship 2 days" (KP 93/1).

[25] NA, RG 84 Honolulu, "Ship's Daily Journal," #7393, where cargo is valued at $3,684; *Honolulu Friend*, n.s. 30, 5 Nov 1881, p. 97.

[26] DAC, 10 Jun 1880; shipping articles, KP 93/6.

[27] NA, RG 84 Honolulu, "Ship's Daily Journal," #7394, 28 Jun 1880-25 Nov 1881. By 1882 Dickson, De Wolf & Co. were dealers in bags and champagne, grain shippers, importers, lumber manufacturers, shipping merchants, and owners of the Hastings sawmill on the mouth of the Burrard Inlet, near the mouth of the Fraser River (Hittel, *Commerce*, pp. 590, 753, 760, 767, 769, 774, 783).

[28] "Statement of master," KP 90/6.

[29] Master of the *Jenny Pitts* in 1868 (*Lewis & Dryden*, 165).

[30] Hittell, *Commerce*, 592.

[31] Legal statement "In re Bark '*Revere*'" in KP 90/7; for disbursements, *see* appendix C.2.

[32] Shipping articles, 28 Feb-1 Mar 1881 (KP 93/1); permission to discharge, KP 92/6; cargo invoice, KP 91/3.

[33] NA, RG 41 San Francisco, permanent enrollment #191, 19 Apr 1881; NA, San Bruno, "Index of enrollments, 1877-1930," vol. 1, p. 236v; shipping articles, 13-21 Apr, KP 93/1; "memo of cargo" from Washington Mill, Seabeck, idem; DAC, 14 Aug 1881.

[34] Charter contract in KP 93/2; insurance policy in KP 90/6; NA, RG 84 Honolulu, "Ship's Daily Journal," #7394; NA, San Bruno, "Index of registers, 1877-1930," vol. 1, 230v; shipping articles, KP 90/6. Williams, Dimond & Co. were San Francisco agents of the Pacific Mail Steamship Co., also importers, shipping merchants, and dealers in engines, oils and rubber goods (Hittell, *History*, 205-6, 764, 770, 772, 780, 783, 784).

Chapter 5

[1] For new contract and insurance, *see* KP 90/6.

[2] Allen & Robinson were the "sole agents for the celebrated Wellington Colliery, Departure Bay," which belonged to Dunsmuir, Diggle (*Honolulu Friend*, n.s. 30, 5 Nov 1881, 96). See also KP 93/2; NA, RG 84 Honolulu, "Ship's Daily Journal," #7395; *Honolulu Friend*, n.s. 31, 1 Jul 1882, 68.

[3] Shipping articles, Port Townsend, 18 Jul-9 Aug, KP 90/8; shipping articles, San Francisco, 24 Aug-4 Sep, KP 93/2; WA, 4 and 11 Aug 1882; NA, RG 36 San Francisco, permanent register #14, 30 Aug 1882; NA San Bruno, "Index of registers, 1877-1930," vol. 1, p. 230; costs in KP 93/2. Waterman & Katz, suppliers in Port Townsend, presented a bill in the amount of $3,093.84.

[4] Shipping articles, Port Townsend, 5 Oct, KP 93/2; NA, RG 84 Honolulu, "Ship's Daily Journal," #7395; WA, 3 Nov, invoices in KP 93/2, 90/8; NA, RG 84 Honolulu, "Ship's Daily Journal," #7395; KP 90/8.

[5] Shipping articles, change of master, District of Puget Sound, 7 April 1883, endorsement in NA, RG 41; see also KP 90/8; NA, RG 84 Honolulu, "Returns of Arrivals and Departures of American Vessels," #7555; WA, 22 Mar, 5 and 12 Apr; *Honolulu Friend*, n.s. 32, 1 Jun 1883, p. 52. For Hinds' command in 1877 (voyage 92), *see* WA, 2 Feb 1877.

[6] Crew list, KP 90/8.

[7] NA, RG 84 Honolulu, "Arrivals and Departures," #7555; *Honolulu Daily Pacific Commercial Advertiser*, 8 Aug-22 Aug.

[8] WA, 7 Oct 1883; wreck report in NA, RG 36.

[9] *San Francisco Examiner*, 9 Jan 1903, p. 13, c. 3, names the seven who were lost with the captain; "a heavy sea prevented saving much from the wreck" (*Lewis & Dryden*, 314).

ABOUT THE AUTHOR

Madeleine Rowse Gleason, a graduate of Smith College, began her career as an instructor in German at her alma mater, after three years of graduate study in Germanic philology at Radcliffe College. Following marriage and a move back to Cambridge she taught German at Cambridge Junior College, but then opted for two part-time jobs: as research assistant and editor to two members of Harvard's history department, specialists with different interests in Tudor and Stuart England. One job ended five years and two volumes later; the other continued until the culmination of two major research projects, in nine published volumes, many years later. She was also co-author with W. K. Jordan of *The Saying of John Late Duke of Northumberland upon the Scaffold, 1553,* and a contributor to the fourth edition of William L. Langer's *Encyclopedia of World History.* In 1972 she was appointed editor of the Harvard Historical Studies and the Harvard Historical Monographs, a position that she held until her retirement in 1980.

At that time Mrs. Gleason took up residence in California and was engaged in freelance editing projects. She had earlier dabbled at tracing the sea-routes of mid-nineteenth century sailing vessels, which came to be a marketable hobby. Her husband's family ship *Revere* was an obvious subject for her attention, and all the more tantalizing when she discovered that the vessel was owned in San Francisco after 1865 and that many of the business records were available at Berkeley. She admits to being addicted to the process of research and uses the original documents when possible to convey the immediacy of the events at hand. The organization of the findings, she says, is a concomitant but necessary evil, "perhaps better delegated to a ghost."

Prior to her retirement Mrs. Gleason had been active in community affairs—an elected member of the Board of Education in Chatham, New Jersey; the director of the Madison-Chatham Adult School; editor for the publications of the local historical societies in Chatham and, later, in Cambridge, where she was also treasurer of the society. She has served as a member of the Friends of the Library Committee at Smith College, as treasurer of her class, and as scholarship chairman for her local club. During her residence in Redwood City, California, she served on the Historic Preservation Board. In the retirement community where she now lives, she has conducted introductory courses in genealogy for residents.

Her next project is a spin-off from the *Revere* research. She is compiling the letters of John Swett, a passenger on the first voyage around Cape Horn, who was a roving reporter for the *Boston Cultivator* during his first years in California, and later the first superintendent of public instruction for the State. He wrote extensive commentaries on life in the mining country, at the San Jose Mission, and expecially in San Francisco, and progressively more about the educational system as it was developing.

BIBLIOGRAPHY

THE MANUSCRIPT SOURCES

The manuscript materials in the National Archives in Washington, D.C., are the *sine qua non* for research in the history of merchant sailing vessels. Documents in the following record groups contain substantial information on the *Revere*:

RG 27, Records of the Weather Bureau, Center for Polar and Scientific Archives: Maury's "abstract log" of the *Revere*, 15 September 1852-29 January 1853 [MS.; Microcopy, M160, 88 Rolls]

RG 36, Records of the Bureau of Customs, Judicial and Fiscal Branch, Civil Archives Division [especially valuable for both Boston and San Francisco shipping, since many records in those ports have been destroyed by fire or by earthquake]:
— Cargo manifests for ports of Baltimore, Mobile, New Orleans, Philadelphia, Seattle [MSS.]
— Passenger lists [microcopy] of vessels arriving at Baltimore (M255), Boston (M277), Mobile (M575), New Orleans (M259), New York (M237)
— Port Townsend, Collector of Customs: wreck report [MS.]
— Returned crew lists, by port [MSS.]

RG 41, Records of the Bureau of Marine Inspection and Navigation, Industrial and Social Branch, Civil Archives Division [MSS.]:
— Bills of sale for registered vessels at Boston, New York, San Francisco [by port, chronologically]
— Certificates of registration and enrollment

RG 59, General Records of the Department of State, Consular Despatches [microcopy]:
Batavia, Java (M449)
Bristol, U.K. (T185)
Callao, Peru (M155)
Canton, China (M101)
Cobija, Bolivia (T381)
Coquimbo, Chile (T332)
Elsinore, Denmark (T201)
Havre, France (T212)
Honolulu, Hawaii (M144)
Leningrad, Russia (M81)
Liverpool, U.K. (M151)
London, U.K. (T168)
Manila, P.I. (T43)
Port Stanley, Falkland Islands (T480)
Rio de Janeiro, Brazil (T172)
St. Helena, West Africa (T428)
St. John, New Brunswick, Canada (T485)
Shanghai, China (M112)
Singapore, Malaya (T128)
Turks Island, B.W.I. (T446)
Valencia, Spain (T447)
Valparaiso, Chile (M146)
Victoria, B.C., Canada (T130)

RG 84, Records of the Foreign Service Posts of the Department of State, Diplomatic Branch, Civil Archives Division [MSS. bound volumes as available for various foreign ports in the following categories]:

— C1.6	Record of fees and declared exports
— C7.2	Copies of ships' registers
— C20	Arrivals and departures of American vessels
— C22	Marine notes of protest
— C23	Marine extended protests
— C24	Ships' daily journals
— C28	Report of American vessels

RG 92, Records of the Office of the Quartermaster General, Navy and Old Army Branch, Military Archives Division: box 88, 10/27/f [MSS.]

RG 241, Records of the Patent and Trademark Office
— Extension case files, s.v. "Frederic Howes" [MSS.]

And in San Bruno, California, among its many documents of the port of San Francisco, the Federal Archives Center holds in RG 36: "Vessels entered coastwise, 1876-1890" (#23); "Certificates of register: 1871, 1875, 1876, 1882-85" (#36), with index (#38); "Articles and crew lists" (#103); "Quarterly returns of masters, 1865-1872" (#106)

Indexes to National Archives Materials:
— "Catalog of National Archives Microfilm Publications, 1974"
— Special Lists, #9, "List of Foreign Service Post Records in the National Archives," from RG 84
— Special List, #22 (2 vols.): "List of American-Flag Merchant Vessels that Received Certificates of Enrollment or Registry at the Port of New York, 1789-1867," from RG 36 and 41

The Kentfield Papers
At the Bancroft Library, University of California, Berkeley. — For the years 1865 to 1883 the Kentfield Papers are indispensable. Of some 115 cartons of papers relating to the business of John Kentfield & Co. from 1854 to 1919, four (#90-93) contain documents pertaining solely to the *Revere*: shipping articles; bills for provisions, repairs, towage and other services, and taxes; cancelled checks; invoices from lumber and coal dealers in Washington Territory and in Nanaimo, B.C.; and Honolulu accounts--all arranged chronologically.

Captain Hamilton's log, 1852-1853
At the G. W. Blunt White Library at Mystic Seaport:—The only known official log of the *Revere* (other than the Maury weather log) in the public domain.

Captain Frederic Howes' logs, 1849-1852
In possession of Leonard H. Dowse, Jr., Hancock, New Hampshire: —Describing Capt. Howes' eight voyages with the *Revere*.

Historical Society of Yarmouth Port, Massachusetts
This organization has several manuscript financial statements pertaining to voyages by Howes & Crowell vessels--among them, three for the *Revere*.

Phelps-Dodge & Co. records
A file, "Correspondence, 1850" (boxes 7-8), is among the Phelps-Dodge holdings in the Manuscript & Archives Section of the New York Public Library. [Voyage 3; not seen.]

Washington Territory company records [not seen]
The Manuscripts and University Archives Division of the University of Washington Libraries in Seattle has records of the Pope and Talbot Company from 1877, including its Puget Mill Company and other subgroups; its archives are at Port Gamble, Washington. Also at the University: records from the Port Blakely Mill Company. Microfilms of the Washington Mill Company papers (1857-1888) are available through Interlibrary Loan.

Printed Materials

Newspapers

The newspapers that published "marine intelligence" are an important adjunct to the documents available in the National Archives. Their columns reported ship arrivals and clearances; news from other ports, both domestic and foreign; and reports on weather, disasters, and sales of ships. With such specific data in hand—the dates, in particular—one is better able to make full use of the vast resources of the archives. A list of abbreviations precedes the notes.

Boston Cultivator
Boston Daily Advertiser
Boston Shipping List and Prices Current
Daily Alta California
Honolulu Friend
London Evening Star
Manchester Guardian
Mobile Daily Register

New Orleans Daily Picayune
New York Journal of Commerce
New York Shipping and Commercial List
Puget Sound Weekly Argus
San Francisco Chronicle
San Francisco Examiner
St. John Morning News

Books and Articles

The Bay of San Francisco . . . A History. 2 vols. Chicago: Lewis
    Publishing Company, 1892.
Bradford, Gershom. *The Mariner's Dictionary.* New York, 1972.
Buchanan, Iva L. "Lumbering and Logging in the Puget Sound Region
    in Territorial Days." In *Pacific Northwest Quarterly* 27 (1936),
    48.
Gilmore, Grant, and Charles L. Black, Jr. *The Law of Admiralty.* Brook-
    lyn: The Foundation Press, 1957.
Gleason, Francis H. "The Revere at Liverpool." In *Antiques* (April
    1979), 795-97.
Gleason, Hall. *Old Ships and Ship-Building Days in Medford.* West
    Medford, MA, 1936.
Hitchman, James H. *The Waterborne Commerce of British Columbia.*
    Occasional Paper#7, Center for Pacific Northwest Studies, West-
    ern Washington State College, 1976.
Hittell, John S. *The Commerce and Industries of the Pacific Coast of
    North America,* etc. San Francisco, 1882.
---. *A History of the City of San Francisco.* San Francisco, 1878.
---. *Resources of California.* Seventh ed., San Francisco, 1879.
Hosburgh, James. *The India Directory, or Directions for Sailing, etc.,*
    Sixth ed., London, 1852.
Howes, Osborn. *An Autobiographical Sketch.* Edited by his children.
    Boston, 1894.
Hunt's Merchants' Magazine and Commercial Review.
Lewis & Dryden's Marine History of the Pacific Northwest. Edited by
    E. W. Wright. Portland: Lewis & Dryden, 1895; reprint, 1961.
Lloyd's *Register of American and Foreign Shipping.*
Lyon, Jane D. *Clipper Ships and Captains.* New York: American Heri-
    tage Junior Library, 1972.

McCurdy, James G. *By Juan de Fuca's Strait.* Portland: Binford's & Mort, 1937.

Morison, Samuel Eliot. *The Maritime History of Massachusetts, 1783-1960.* Cambridge, 1961.

Professional and Industrial History of Suffolk County, Massachusetts. Vol. 2, Boston, 1899.

Prosser, William Farrand. *A History of Puget Sound Country.* 2 vols., Lewis Publishing Co., 1903.

Rutter, Frank R. "The South American Trade of Baltimore." In *Johns Hopkins University Studies in Historical and Political Science,* ser. 15, no. 9 (Sep 1897): 371-451 [sep. pag. 7-87].

San Francisco city directories.

Soulé, Frank. *The Annals of San Francisco.* Facsimile ed., Palo Alto, 1966.

Swett, John. *Public Education in California . . . with Personal Reminiscences.* New York, 1911.

U.S. Hydrographic Office. *Navigation of the Caribbean Sea and the Gulf of Mexico.* Publication #86, vol. 1, 1888.

Weidberg, Dorothy. "The History of John Kentfield and Company, 1854-1925." Typescript, M.A. thesis, U. Cal. Berkeley, 1940.

Whidden, Captain John D. *Ocean Life in the Old Sailing Ship Days.* Boston: Little, Brown & Company, 1909.

Winsor, Justin. *Memorial History of Boston.* 4 vols., Boston, 1883.

INDEX